Corwin A. Bennett is Professor of Industrial Engineering at Kansas State University. With degrees in industrial and experimental psychology, he has had extensive experience in both industry and education, working in management, planning, research, development, and teaching.

SPACES FOR PEOPLE
Human Factors in Design

Corwin Bennett

A SPECTRUM BOOK

PRENTICE-HALL, INC., Englewood Cliffs, New Jersey 07632

Library of Congress Cataloging in Publication Data

Bennett, Corwin.
　　Spaces for people.

　　(A Spectrum Book)
　　Includes bibliographies and index.
　　1. Architecture—Human factors.　　I. Title.
NA2542.4.B46　　　　721　　　76-30847
ISBN 0-13-823963-0
ISBN 0-13-823955-X pbk.

© 1977 by Prentice-Hall, Inc., Englewood Cliffs, N.J. 07632

All rights reserved. No part of this book may
be reproduced in any form or by any means without
permission in writing from the publisher.

A Spectrum Book

Printed in the United States of America

10　9　8　7　6　5　4　3　2　1

Prentice-Hall International, Inc., *London*
Prentice-Hall of Australia Pty. Limited, *Sydney*
Prentice-Hall of Canada, Ltd., *Toronto*
Prentice-Hall of India Private Limited, *New Delhi*
Prentice-Hall of Japan, Inc., *Tokyo*
Prentice-Hall of Southeast Asia Pte. Ltd., *Singapore*
Whitehall Books Limited, *Wellington, New Zealand*

Contents

Dedication and Acknowledgments   viii

Preface   ix

I
INTRODUCTION

1
Interior Spaces: A Man-Environment Interface   3

2
Designing for Human What?: Design/Evaluation Criteria   11

II
DESIGNING

3
Individual Spaces   27

4
Smaller Spaces   58

5
Larger Spaces   69

III
ENVIRONMENTAL EFFECTS

6
The Luminous Environment   87

7
The Sound Environment   113

8
The Thermal Environment   127

IV
PUTTING IT ALL TOGETHER

9
Research and Design   **139**

10
Creativity and Problem Solving   **162**

11
Presenting the Design   **177**

Index   **183**

Dedication and Acknowledgments

I wish to acknowledge the support of and dedicate this book to my wife, family, and self, for whom it has been done. To my many fine teachers, especially Frank Dudek of the University of Nebraska. To my many colleagues in human factors, especially to Merritt Olson of the Rand Corporation; and to Paule Rey of the University of Geneva, who sold the interior ergonomics course at Kansas State. To the students of interior design and architecture and the readers of *Environmental Design News* for the chance to develop my ideas.

Specific thanks are given to Stephan Konz of Kansas State University for reviewing Chapter 8 on the thermal environment and to C. L. Crouch of the Illuminating Engineering Research Institute for reviewing an early version of Chapter 6 on the luminous environment. Appreciation is due to Harrison Gough for permission to use the brief creativity test. Thanks are given to Marie Davis, who typed most of the manuscript. I appreciate having the material in Table 3.2 provided by Wesley Woodson.

Preface

"Let's design for people." That's what a reviewer said this book is about. Ergonomics, or human factors, is about designing for people. The field started with a concern for designing military hardware to fit people, but ergonomic interests have broadened. For example, the Human Factors Society of the United States has an interest group concerned with design of the built environment that is largely concerned with interior spaces. Although designers do design for people, they need specialized knowledge and sometimes assistance to carry this out.

This book is intended for any designer of interior spaces, whether the practicing professional, the student—of interior design or of architecture—or the amateur who is going to do some design. In general, the object is *not* to tell someone *how* to design, although there is some material of this sort in Part II. It is assumed that formal interior design coursework and experience teach design. Rather, this book is meant to present what may be additional knowledge on accommodating people *while* designing. Certain auxiliary, nondesign topics of importance to the designer are also included.

It is traditional to refer to abstract people, such as "the chemist" as he or him. In the light of contemporary thinking about roles of the sexes this seems rather arbitrary. I have consistently referred to the designer as she or her, and to others as he or him. Many designers of interior spaces are women, and certainly most of my students are.

Inevitably, there are errors, misstatements, and omissions in this book.

Furthermore, as there are different approaches to and illustrations of the topic, the author would appreciate receiving your comments on this presentation.

1
Introduction

This section deals with two topics. First it explores the nature and relations of the interior space design discipline and the ergonomics, or human factors, discipline. This book concerns how ergonomics can help the interior space designer satisfy human user needs. The second topic of this section is the definition of those human needs—the objectives or criteria toward which one should design and by which a design should be evaluated. These goals are health and safety, performance, comfort, and aesthetic pleasantness, the criteria that will be used throughout the book.

1

Interior Spaces: A Man-Environment Interface

"We do most of our living indoors."

CORWIN BENNETT

With technological development, design has become more complex. This complexity has placed greater burdens on the designer and created the need for specialists to support particular aspects of design. "Ergonomics" or "human factors" is concerned with designing to meet the needs of human users. It draws on disciplines such as psychology and physiology for information and techniques. Part of the ergonomic contribution to design is new research on how particular aspects of the built environment affect people. The initial section of this book deals with the general process of design and design criteria to satisfy human needs. A further section deals with design of spaces for varying numbers of people. Principal environmental aspects of interior spaces are considered. Finally, various activities of the designer, necessary to designing, presenting the design, and evaluating the design, are included.

Building design has become more complex.

DESIGN COMPLEXITY AND SPECIALIZATION

Thomas Jefferson not only designed the University of Virginia campus and its buildings but also planned the curriculum and selected books for the library. About 200 years later, the university department of which this writer is a member moved into a new building designed not only by a team of designing architects but also by several engineers and "supervising state architects," with inputs from a number of University personnel. While part of the increase in personnel may be due to the scarcity of Thomas Jeffersons, the complexity of buildings has increased considerably. The 100-year-old university building that was replaced had originally no plumbing or electricity. The present building has several types of electrical service—dimmable lights, air conditioning, compressed air service, specialized ventilation, and so on.

Architecture has focused on exterior building appearances.

Although a recent book claiming to deal with architecture and people included a chapter dealing with "the design team," no one particularly concerned with the design of interiors was mentioned. It may be that the architect gives as much attention to the interior design as to the exterior design and therefore needs no specialist. Frequently, however, it may be otherwise, as in the design of one particular building. The architect first presented a perspective of the exterior, a mirrored, twentieth-century castle, as it were. Some time later, floor planning was done. This is, of course, contrary to the dictum of the eminent American architect, Louis Sullivan, who said that form should follow function—advice frequently not taken.

New specialties have developed.

During and after World War II various new specialties within engineering design developed, such as human factors (ergonomics), and maintainability engineering. The competent engineering designer has always been concerned with designing equipment to be operated effectively and repaired readily. But the ergonomic and maintainability specialists by virtue of their specialization have developed bodies of knowledge and expertise in their areas that have gone beyond the scope of the designing engineer.

In the same way, interior space design specialities will blossom forth. Interior space designers can focus their efforts to develop a body of knowledge and expertise beyond that of the generalized architect. The popular image has perhaps been that of the interior decorator who worked for a store and who at the behest of a housewife would redo her home in the products of the store. In contrast, interior design is developing as a profession whose practitioners receive at least baccalaureate training in many aspects of the design of interior spaces. Some of these programs have added special training in ergonomics or human factors.

Interior space design permits new expertise.

ERGONOMICS

Ergonomics (a British term meaning laws of work) or *human factors* (an American term referring largely to "operability" engineering—designing for the operator or user) started during World War II as an approach to prevent accidents and foster better human performance with highly complicated military equipment, especially aircraft. Although such work remains an important field of application, many practitioners are now primarily concerned with civil pursuits such as industrial operations, consumer products, and the built environment.

Ergonomics is concerned with design for humans.

Our focus on the "built environment" may be set off by a quotation from Morrison: ". . . at the very moment when by our wit we have developed the means to give us considerable control over our resistant natural environment we find we have produced in the means themselves an artificial environment of such complication that we cannot control it . . . ." While this may bring up visions of environmental pollution, and problems of transportation, energy, and housing,

Most living is done indoors.

a critical aspect of the built environment is that of building interiors. *Most of us live and work most of the time in interiors.* If we are poisoned by air contamination or deafened by noise it is most likely to happen indoors. We perform our work as housewives or employees inside. As we are indoors most of the time we are made comfortable or uncomfortable by the temperature, the seating, and the other conditions indoors. Although we may occasionally get out into beautiful outdoor areas, most of our aesthetic experience is determined by our homes, offices, and factories. If they are ugly, how will this condition our lives?

Interior ergonomics is based on several sciences.

Interior ergonomics is concerned with designing interior spaces so that the various needs of the users will be best fulfilled. Ergonomics draws on the knowledge of the human sciences and technologies as they apply to design. Psychology, for example, provides information on how well people can see detail and therefore implies how large characters on signs should be. Recent studies in social psychology tell about how people like to sit in relation to others whom they know, don't know, wish to talk to, or want privacy from. Physiology tells of some of the mechanisms underlying discomfort in seating and glare. Anthropometry gives numbers on the sizes of people so that one can decide how high to make a table. Industrial engineering has developed practical techniques for floor planning.

Applied research can answer design questions.

Beyond the large bodies of knowledge that have built up in the sciences, some of which is useful to the designer, the research tradition and research know-how of the sciences will be important to the designer in the future. Only in the past few years has there been any general recognition of the possibility of doing research on interior design questions. Design was strictly an art and, as in other arts, what was good was presumably known to the designer, though she might not know why. Or, in a more sophisticated way, various intuitively known laws or principles might direct the designer to good design. The so-called laws of color harmony advocated that in using two hues one should use either the same hues or strongly contrasting hues to achieve pleasantness. The empirical research of Helson (1970) has enlarged this rule. There are in fact hue combinations at various distances apart along the light spectrum which produce pleasantness.

Another kind of research which has come on in design in recent years is space evaluation. Although some research questions are very difficult to test, such as "Are aesthetically pleasing classrooms better?", we can evaluate specific designs: "In this classroom, which was designed to be aesthetically pleasing, did students learn more?"

Evaluation research tests specific designs.

REVIEW OF THE BOOK

In the next chapter we shall consider the various human objectives of design. These are health and safety, performance, comfort, and aesthetic pleasantness.

In Part II designing for humans is considered on three levels. First, the design of individual spaces such as seats and desks is considered from the standpoint of people's sizes and their seeing and manipulating capabilities. Then, spaces for a few people are examined from the viewpoint of desired social activities. Finally, the design of spaces for a large number of people and their equipment is considered primarily with the goal of achieving efficiency of interaction among parts of an organization.

Designing different-sized spaces is considered.

Part III deals with the effects of the environment on people and the implications for the design of interior spaces. Most important to the designer is lighting. By proper lighting she can not only avoid nega-

Aspects of the interior environment are considered.

tive effects such as glare but also create positive results such as good performance and pleasantness. The sound and thermal environments present design goals that are largely negative: avoiding annoyance or discomfort.

In the final section several auxiliary topics are considered. Specific types of research related to interior design are described. Creativity and problem-solving, critical aspects of design, are analyzed. Finally, the important matter of presenting the design in such a way that it can be understood and accepted is discussed.

Research, creativity, and presenting are discussed.

THE DESIGN-EVALUATION CYCLE

Designing and related activities discussed in this book can be seen in Figure 1.1. Here designing is seen as a creative and problem-solving process.

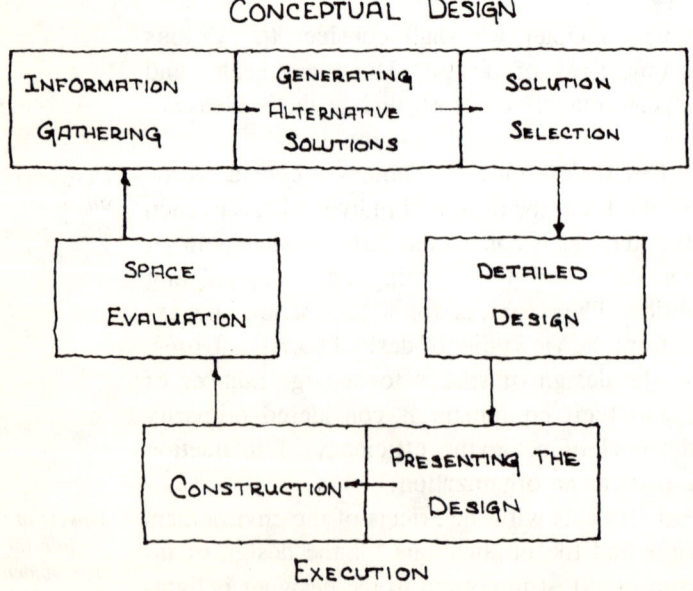

Figure 1.1 *The design-evaluation cycle.*

Information must be gathered on the objectives for the space and the nature of the activities to be performed in it. The creative process of generating a number of potential, alternative solutions is next. Finally, some problem-solving or decision-making steps must be gone through to select a viable solution and/or a best solution.

The selection of a solution may be identical with doing an analytical evaluation. For example, in the design of large spaces (floor planning), the degree to which each alternative solution meets the design requirements in terms of ease of interaction among activities can be *calculated*. Based on these calculations, the relative functional merit of the several solutions can be an important part of selecting a solution. Detailed design can then be undertaken, completing the design work.

The design must be presented to the client. Presentation is as much a part of the execution of the project as actual construction. Once the space is built and occupied (granted some "settling-in" period) it can be evaluated. This evaluation may be a basis for the modification of this space to correct problems. Space evaluation may also be the basis for modifying the designer's approach to some future design project. Otherwise the designer, as Wools (1970) puts it, might be "likened to a cuckoo who does not come back to roost—he doesn't revisit his buildings after they're built" (and presumably keeps making the same errors over and over).

Now, I suggest you go back and read the summary at the beginning of the chapter.

DISCUSSION

1. When an artist draws or paints a building, why is it more likely to be an older building rather than a contemporary building?

2. When an artist draws or paints a building, why is his subject more likely to be the outside of the building rather than the inside?

EXERCISE

In terms of your design experience, what questions have you had about the topics of this book that concern designing for people. What would you like to know?

REFERENCES

HELSON, H., and T. LANSFORD. The role of spectral energy of source and background color in the pleasantness of object colors. *Applied Optics,* 9; 1513-1562, 1970.

WOOLS, R. M. The assessment of room friendliness. In D. V. CANTER (ED). *Architectural psychology.* London: Royal Institute of British Architects, 1970.

2

Designing for Human What? Design / Evaluation Criteria

"Opulence was mistakenly defined as good taste."

H.J. BONELLIE

Design is difficult because it must satisfy several criteria. These design (and evaluation) criteria constitute a hierarchy. First a space must be safe and healthy. A space must enable users to perform their functions. A design should not cause discomfort. Finally, a design should be aesthetically pleasing.

Design is a difficult process, for one reason, because good design attempts to satisfy several goals simultaneously. Who would want to be responsible for a space that was unsafe or unhealthy, did not permit its intended function to be fulfilled, or was uncomfortable or ugly? The designer explicitly or implicitly tries to avoid all these errors.

Good design tries to meet several goals.

These design objectives are not equal, however. They form a hierarchy, and sometimes designers or clients are willing to have only those goals early in the hierarchy satisfied, ignoring the others (Bennett, 1972). An executive of a company building a new factory, for example, may dictate, "I want it safe and healthy, and most of all I want the workers to be able

Design goals form a hierarchy.

to perform efficiently." He might have added, "If you can make it comfortable and pleasant at no extra cost, okay." He may have thought about comfort, but the idea of pleasantness might never have occurred to him except in relation to certain public areas frequently exposed to visitors. (In general, in commercial spaces, pleasantness is desired where it will impress customers. In bureaucracies it is used to demonstrate the importance of an officeholder.)

SAFETY / HEALTH

Keep the user safe and healthy.

Although we might separate the criteria of safety and health, it is convenient to pair them. The U.S. Occupational Safety and Health Act (OSHA) set as an objective a safe and healthy environment for every worker (Department of Labor, 1971). Similarly, the interior space designer must have as a goal the safety and health of each user of her space. One reaction of designers is, "Oh, well, that's taken care of by the building code" (or, perhaps by OSHA). Government regulations, of course, are there to protect the user and worker. However, it is actually the designer who makes space healthy and safe.

Environmental health problems are mainly in factories.

In interiors, most health problems other than those brought about through complex psychological mechanisms are found in factories. Very common problems are those due to exposing occupants to harmful substances through air contamination or by contact with harmful liquids. Closed and automated systems that prevent contact with the poisons are the general solution. Other health threats come from extreme conditions of noise, heat, and cold, also principally in factories.

Safety hazards are widespread.

Safety implications are more widespread, although factory-type environments may be more severe. People can fall down stairs or be electrocuted in any type of interior. In fact, home accidents account for about twice the number of accidental deaths and injuries of those in paid workplaces. Of the various means for achieving safety, most important is accident prevention through good design. One can put up warning signs for a dangerous step or a low overhang. Much better is the elimination of the hazard—directly, or by keeping pedestrians away.

Good design is the key to health and safety. Except in extreme environments where a calculated risk may be taken, safety and health come before performance, comfort, or pleasantness.

Design is the key to health and safety.

PERFORMANCE

We not only want to keep the occupants alive and unharmed, we want them to be able to perform their intended functions. A home is built to enable people to cook, eat, sleep, and so on. Obviously, business places are designed so that people can perform their jobs.

Buildings are built to do something in.

In factories, the principle which industrial engineering learned years ago was that the individual workplace must be designed so that the individual job can be performed well. Then, you need to arrange the workplaces so that the total job can be performed well. Homes, offices, and stores are the same. Thus, workplace design and floor planning are the key positive aspects to making a space "functional."

Workplace design and floor planning are keys.

How about the comfort and pleasantness of the space? Don't they help people perform better? We will discuss this further, but, in general, the answer is "no." Comfort and pleasantness are ends in themselves, not means to good performance.

On the negative side, poor environmental conditions may hurt performance. This is certainly true of bad lighting. Noise may interfere with speech per-

A poor environment may hinder performance.

formance. Poor temperature, however, hot or cold, has little performance effect except at extremes that are not commonly encountered in interiors.

Put things where they belong.

Designing for performance thus is largely designing for "convenience," for suitability for people and machines—putting things where they need to be. Some hardheaded bosses would not like the term "convenience" because it implies ease to the worker also. However, a job can be uncomfortable, which may be a sign that it can't be performed well.

COMFORT

There are many sources of discomfort.

Just about anything people come into contact with can be uncomfortable—lighting (glare), sound (annoying noise), seats, other furniture, thermal conditions. Generally we are trying to prevent discomfort rather than create comfort. (On the positive side we try to create pleasantness.) Why is there discomfort? Physiologically, there are as many answers as there are types of discomfort. At least one reason that light can be glaringly uncomfortable is the sudden closing down of the pupils of the eyes. In seat discomfort, it is generally too much pressure on some of the supporting parts of the body.

Discomfort protects us against extremes.

In general, however, comfort seems to fulfill a biological function. The function of discomfort is to protect the person from more extreme conditions. For example, a range of a few degrees of temperature (and other thermal conditions) is comfortable for most people. Call this the "thermal comfort" range. Extend the temperature out of this range and people become increasingly uncomfortable. They still can perform tasks satisfactorily. We might call this the "thermal performance" range. Extend the temperature even further, up or down. People's work performance will deteriorate, and eventually their health and safety will be threatened. But stop, go back! When the temperature became uncomfortable, what did people do? If possible, they changed it. They reduced the heat or reduced the cold or left the space to protect themselves against the possibility of worse consequences than discomfort. Similarly, hardly anyone will look at the sun for more than a moment, which protects us against retinal damage. Some discomfort is not so protective because normally a long exposure is required to damage the body. One occasion of sitting, even for hours, in a misfitting seat won't produce back problems. Many occasions might. For most harmful noise levels, one exposure will produce only temporary loss of hearing. Months or years are usually required for permanent loss. People tend to resign themselves to the discomfort, ignoring its protective function.

As technology has developed, our tolerance of discomfort has declined. Before the advent of electric lighting people sometimes worked under such poor illumination that they were probably uncomfortable much of the time. With the development of electric lighting, and improved electric lighting, it became possible to provide better and higher illumination. Indeed, some critics have remarked on the increase in illumination standards as though they were contrived to sell electricity. They *were* contrived (designed by man) to enable people to see better. Similarly, heating and cooling systems and other artifacts have developed for comfort. Most offices in the United States today are air conditioned. In 1930 they weren't. Why not? Effective, economical air conditioning equipment didn't exist. As it was developed it was used more extensively, first in recreational places—theaters and restaurants—and then in homes and offices. Today people expect certain types of spaces to be thermally comfortable. If their expectations are not met, they notice it and are distracted.

We are becoming less tolerant of discomfort.

Discomfort may be distracting.

Indeed, the British engineer Corlett (1973), has suggested that discomfort occurs when one is distracted from the task at hand. If one is distracted from watching television or typing a letter, discomfort has taken place and produced a performance problem. It may be that the greater provision for comfort has more closely linked comfort and performance—not through the physiological bases of discomfort, but through the psychological mechanism of distraction.

AESTHETIC PLEASANTNESS

Pleasantness is a multi-dimensional criterion.

Whereas comfort is largely a negative issue—how to prevent discomfort—pleasantness is a positive goal. In all the design evaluation criteria—safety, health, performance, and comfort—there are multiple aspects to the goals. There are various threats to health and safety; various tasks to perform, each with more than one aspect of goodness; and several kinds of discomfort. For none of the criteria is this multidimensionality more evident than for aesthetic pleasantness. A design theorist might say that the dimensions of pleasantness are scale, proportion, harmony, and the like. But we must wonder: Have we covered everything? Are the dimensions independent?

Pleasantness dimensions include evaluation, organization, and spaciousness.

In the past few years several "semantic differential" studies of subjective reactions to buildings and spaces have been conducted. Observers rate the space on a number of scales, such as beautiful-ugly, neat-messy, spacious-crowded. The ratings are statistically correlated and factor-analyzed into a few factors or dimensions. For example, Seaton and Collins (1972) reviewed several such studies and concluded that each found a general evaluation dimension (e.g., pleasant-unpleasant), an organization dimension (e.g., orderly-disorderly), and a spaciousness dimension (e.g., uncluttered-cluttered).

In the author's own research on public and private campus spaces, the aesthetic evaluation factor was "loaded" with characteristics like "contemporary" and "carpeted." A major factor distinguishing these particular spaces was a privacy-quiet factor (contrasting offices with lobbies, etc.). The spaciousness factor broke into two dimensions—some spaces are roomy and uncluttered simply because they have few furnishings. Some spaces are roomy and uncluttered because they have furnishings—closets, tables and so forth—built in.

Other dimensions of pleasantness have been found.

These semantic differential studies, like the design theorist's list, are interesting. They tell us how people in general react to various aspects of the built environment. Generally, however, they do not tell the designer what to do. "Spaces evaluated highly are pleasant, beautiful, interesting, and exciting. So how do I achieve these things?"

Rating studies don't tell how to design.

Other work is going on. For example, some experimental research tests which design features give the feeling of spaciousness. The author (1975) is doing correlational research to find out what objective (denotative) indicators in offices and living rooms—use of drapes and carpeting, furniture density—are associated with the various (connotative) semantic dimensions.

SEMANTIC DIFFERENTIAL

C. E. Osgood (1957), a University of Illinois psychologist, and his associates developed the *semantic differential* to evaluate concepts. Judges rate words, concepts, or ideas on a large number of descriptive scales. These scales are anchored at each end by opposites such as good-bad, strong-weak, and fast-slow. Since its conception, the semantic differential has been used in thousands of studies in many languages and countries. One result has been the finding in many such studies of the same three-dimensional "meaning" or "connotative space." The first and most important dimension is the *evaluative* one represented by terms like "good" and "bad." The most important thing we can (and do) say about something is that it is good or bad (or that we like it or not). Two lesser dimensions are *potency* (strong-weak) and *activity* (fast-slow). Some sample words or concepts in terms of the three-dimensional semantic structure are shown below. Here the positive numbers represent good, strong, and fast; and negative numbers represent the converse. A value of "one" or "two" should be considered substantial:

Idea	Evaluation	Potency	Activity
woman	1.9	0.4	1.1
man	1.3	1.5	0.6

Thus, women are judged "better" than men but less "powerful" and more "active." These results, clearly, are not a woman's liberationist viewpoint.

army	1.4	2.2	1.1

A pre-Vietnam judgment.

love	2.3	2.4	0.6
sex	2.0	2.1	0.7

While the differences between "love" and "sex" are in expected directions it is interesting how little difference there is in the eyes of these college-student judges.

student	1.3	0.9	1.0
professor	1.1	0.7	0.1 (!)

In applying the semantic differential to the built environment, a common question has been, "Do the three dimensions apply to things as well as to words?" In almost all cases a large evaluation factor emerges. The other two dimensions do not arise as clearly. In the author's work with public and private spaces, "activity" factors emerged—"private," "quiet," "slow," "personal," "closed," and the like. A clear-cut potency factor was not there. In a study of lighting of lecture halls, Hopkinson (1971) found an "evaluation" factor and a "potency" factor ("light," "strong," "bright," and so on). An activity factor was not so obvious. Our conclusion on the whether the three dimensions are applicable is "yes and no."

Pleasantness may produce other subjective effects. Psychologists Maslow and Mintz (1956), had people judge photographs of faces, sometimes in a pleasant room, sometimes in an "average" one, and sometimes in an unpleasant one. Although some judgments were unaffected, faces were judged higher in energy and well-being in the more pleasant rooms. However, judges were apparently not consciously sensitive to the condition of the rooms. Such a study should be replicated.

Judgments were affected by room pleasantness.

An eminent architect designed a new state university campus in New York. It was intended to be beautiful. Indeed it was impressive—with five towered clusters of buildings—from the air. A number of serious design faults hampered performance, however. When questioned on this the architect replied, "It's so beautiful they won't notice." That may be so for the casual visitor, but not for the user. It's as if the designer were designing a wife for a man. She gives her appealing external features, e.g., a sexy figure, but neglects her temperament and competence. Unfortunately, the client who is less able to assess the other criteria of design may be over-influenced by pleasantness.

Pleasantness is no substitute for other characteristics.

BEYOND PLEASANTNESS

Other design evaluation criteria could be listed, for example, economy. Here we have focused on the

There are other design criteria.

criteria of immediate application to the users of the space. Doing an otherwise good design cheaply is obviously desirable for most clients.

Motives may form a hierarchy.

Maslow (1954) postulated a hierarchy of needs (human motivations) ranging from physiological needs such as for food through the need for security, the need to belong, and the need for prestige, to "self-actualization"—the need to express one's full potentialities. The "lower" needs would have to be fulfilled before there would be concern for higher needs. Analogously, safety comes before pleasantness.

Actualization is sometimes a goal.

Also in some kinds of design, such as the design of jobs and games, we can speak of actualizability. A challenging job stretches the person to his utmost and gives him rich satisfaction in its accomplishment. It is actualizing. A "rich" game like bridge, poker, or chess challenges and rewards the novice or the expert. Can spaces lead to actualization? Permit it? Is actualization in this realm an analogue to the aesthetic pleasantness of the built environment?

A good design satisfies all criteria.

To return to our initial theme: The various design evaluation goals form a hierarchy. If a space threatens one's safety and health, who wants to risk it? If a space doesn't permit performance, who needs it? If it isn't comfortable, who wants to tolerate it? (An architect describing a beautiful but hellishly hot building in Barcelona said, "Who can speak of aesthetics at 120°?") If the space isn't beautiful, who wants it? A good design satisfies all criteria.

Reread the chapter summary.

DISCUSSION

1. To what extent do (should) the various criteria apply to different types of artifacts—homes, offices, factories, cars, bull dozers, etc.?

2. The (Protestant or Puritan) work ethic includes the idea that

one should work hard ("Conscientious performance of one's labor is man's highest duty," said Martin Luther). Confounded with this is the idea that work should be disagreeable and therefore work places should be uncomfortable and unpleasant (like the idea that medicine should taste bad or sting in order to be effective). Many workplaces, especially factories are, indeed, unpleasant. What about it?

EXERCISE: PLEASANTNESS RATINGS

Select some spaces which are personally interesting or which you think have extreme characteristics. Visit them if possible. First list the characteristics of the space which you feel are most distinctive (such as, "The furniture is rotten."). Now rate each space on each of the following scales:

(E) Interesting			Average			Uninteresting
7	6	5	4	3	2	1
(O) Disorderly			Average			Orderly
1	2	3	4	5	6	7
(S) Roomy			Average			Not Roomy
7	6	5	4	3	2	1
(E) Unpleasant			Average			Pleasant
1	2	3	4	5	6	7
(O) Neat			Average			Messy
7	6	5	4	3	2	1
(S) Crowded			Average			Spacious
1	2	3	4	5	6	7
(E) Beautiful			Average			Ugly
7	6	5	4	3	2	1
(O) Untidy			Average			Tidy
1	2	3	4	5	6	7
(S) Uncluttered			Average			Cluttered
7	6	5	4	3	2	1

Combine the ratings from several people as follows:
1. Each judge should make all ratings of spaces independent of others' opinions on the scales provided.

2. Determine the *median* rating by the judges for each pair of terms (each scale). The median is the middle score. Thus, if there were an odd number of scores, pick the middle one. If there were five scores, say, 2, 2, 3, 5, 7, the median would be "3." If there were an even number of scores, the median would be halfway between the middle two. If there were four scores, say, 2, 3, 6, 7, the median would be 4.5.
3. Add the three median scores labeled "E" (evaluation), that is, "interesting," "pleasant," and "beautiful." Divide this sum by three. Do the same for the three medians for "O" (orderliness) and "S" (spaciousness). You now have an average score for each dimension.
4. Consider any rating between 3 and 5 "average," above 5 "high," and below 3 "low."

Now how do the characteristics which you earlier listed seem to relate to these ratings?

REFERENCES

BENNETT, C. A. Designing for human what? *Human Factors Bulletin,* 15(2):3, 1972.

BENNETT, C. A. Objective indicators for predicting dimensions of architectural pleasantness. In *Proceedings of Conference on Environmental Effects on Behavior,* Big Sky, Montana, July 1975.

CORLETT, E. N. Human factors in the design of manufacturing systems. *Human Factors,* 15(2), 105-110, 1973.

DEPARTMENT OF LABOR. Occupational safety and health standards. *Federal Register,* 36 (105), Part II, 1971.

HOPKINSON, R. and WATSON, N. A study of lighting quality. Unpublished report, London, 1971.

MASLOW, A., and N. L. MINTZ. The effects of esthetic surroundings. *Journal of Psychology,* 41: 247-254, 1956.

MINTZ, N. L. Effects of esthetic surroundings: II. Prolonged and repeated experience in a "beautiful" and "ugly" room, *Journal of Psychology,* 41:459-466, 1956.

OSGOOD, C. E., G. J. SUCI, and P. H. TANNEUBAUM, *The measurement of meaning*. Urbana: University of Illinois, 1957.

SEATON, R. W., and J. B. COLLINS, Validity and reliability of ratings of simulated buildings. *In Proceedings of the EDRA 3 Conference,* Los Angeles, January 1972.

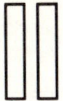

Designing

This section is concerned with the design of furnishings and spaces for human users. In Chapter 3, Individual Spaces, we first look at anthropometry, the measurement of people's physical characteristics. These are then applied to the design of furniture, especially to seats and workplaces. Chapters 4 and 5 deal with designing spaces. The design of smaller spaces involving only a handful of people depends largely on social considerations. The design of larger spaces involving many people and much equipment depends primarily on the functions to be performed within the spaces and the interrelations among their functions.

3

Individual Spaces

"The most important thing that psychology has to say is that people are different."

Anthropometry is concerned primarily with the measurement of various body dimensions. Distributions of such data can then be used by the designer to design or select furniture. Seating design for sitting comfort is considered in detail. A fundamental design principle to achieve sitting comfort is to spread the weight of the body over as great an area as possible. In designing an individual's workplace it is generally important to provide for good seeing in terms of viewing angles and distances. The optimal hand activity area is defined as being slightly below elbow height. Using this fact plus anthropometric data, sitting and standing work-surface heights and seats are defined. The hardware of a space should also be selected by the designer to be functional.

ANTHROPOMETRY

Anthropometry (the measurement of man) is a part of physical anthropology. It was developed as a tool for

Knowing the sizes of people is useful.

distinguishing racial groups. For example, the ratio of head length (or depth) to head breadth was used to separate some groups—some people being long-headed, some wide-headed. Eventually it was realized that knowing the distribution of sizes of people had other useful purposes. For example, as a child the author was one of many children measured to establish a better basis for children's clothing sizes. During World War II the military services did extensive measuring of people, not only for clothing but also for equipment design. Later anthropometry served the space program in the design of space suits and astronaut support systems.

Influencing Factors

Size changes with age.

Many factors influence body size. Foremost of these is age, reflected in the remarkable growth of the body during the first two decades of life. Specialized data can be found for various groups. Notable is the work of H. W. Oxford (1969), who determined six chair sizes suitable for accommodating boys and girls through primary and secondary school. After the growth of youth, in societies where food is overabundant, there is continued growth in weight, which changes various body dimensions. In the last few decades of life there may be another gradual change—a loss of stature (standing height). Most of the evidence on this point is inconclusive because it is based on measures of age groups made up of different people rather than the same people at different ages. Thus, if 70-year-olds are shorter than 50-year-olds, it is not possible to determine whether they became shorter as they aged, or whether those born 20 years earlier were shorter at comparable ages.

There are slow and fast changes in body size.

There are some other time-dependent, non-age-related changes in body size. As is well known, people are getting larger, both taller and heavier. Over centuries the change has been dramatic, from armor wearers to armored-car drivers, almost a foot in average height. Within the lifetime of living persons in the U.S., height has probably increased more than an inch. In general such slow changes don't concern the designer. Some very fast changes do take place in height however. During the course of a day we all get shorter by a fraction of an inch. When we get up in the morning, the cartilaginous discs that make up part of the spinal column are thick, making us taller. As the day wears on, the weight of the body on the spine compresses the discs. As they become thinner, we become slightly shorter.

Obviously there are distinct differences between the sexes in body dimensions. U.S. women average 5'3" (159 cm.) in height, men 5'8" (172 cm.); thus average adults are 5'5" (166 cm.). Not only are there important differences in height, weight, and most body dimensions, but also there are behavioral consequences. Brookes found that because of their shorter arm length and different weight distribution the climbing of utility poles by women required that they have disproportionately *greater* strength than men. Because most anthropometric data has been gathered by the military services, which have long practiced sex discrimination, there are fewer data available on women than on men.

There are sex differences!

Various social group differences are associated with anthropometric differences. Well-known are size differences among nationalities and presumably races. Americans are among the largest peoples of the world. West Europeans are quite large. Orientals are smaller. Imported foreign cars have been even more cramped than American cars. The smaller peoples are not, however, just scaled-down versions of larger peoples. Orientals have relatively long torsos and short limbs. Japanese shirts "in the same size" tend to have long

There are social group differences.

bodies and tails compared to American-made garments. A further social group difference is in social class. Among men, at least in the U.S. and probably in most cultures, large size, especially height, is an advantage. Large stature is helpful in most sports, and it is believed also to be helpful in selling. Executives also tend to be taller than other employees. American college men average 6'0" (182 cm.) compared to the average 5'8" (172 cm.) for American men in general.

Distributions and Design

Design for some large percent of the people.

Although it is convenient to summarize the distribution of some body sizes by a mean size (as we have been doing), for most design purposes this single figure is inadequate. In general, the designer should select some percentage of her population (for instance, 95 percent) and design to accommodate it. For example, suppose a console is intended to be low enough for seated people to see over. The mean sitting eye height for a 16-inch (41 cm.) high seat is about 46 inches (117 cm.) from the floor. But if we design the console to be 46 inches high, then fully *half* of the population would not be able to see over it easily! If we set the height equal to that of the smallest 5 percent of the population, that is, at 44 inches (112 cm.), then 95 percent should be able to see over it readily. In some cases it is so inexpensive to accommodate a large fraction of the population that we extend this common 95 percent design goal and design for almost everyone. The standard 6'8" (203 cm.) door height is tall enough for more than 99% of the population.

In general, in designing furniture for people we need to do one of three things: (1) make it so large or so small that it accommodates most people, or (2) make it adjustable, or (3) make several sizes so that a proper one can be selected for a given person. Keep these alternatives in mind!

Some Anthropometric Data

Many anthropometric studies have been carried out on a variety of U.S. and other groups. Although more up-to-date studies on more representative civilian populations are needed, the existing data are useful. A variety of body measures have been made in the different studies. Of the several compilations of anthropometric data, one of the best is by Hertzberg (1972), formerly a U.S. Air Force anthropometrist. These data include measures of strength of various parts of the body and degrees of movement of various joints.

In Table 3.1 a very brief summary of body sizes is given. Figure 3.1 shows the location of these dimensions on the human body. Except for weight in pounds, which is given in kilograms in parenthesis, all linear measures are given in inches, with centimeters in parentheses.

When available, five different percentage measures are given for women, for men, and for both sexes. The "50%" numbers, the 50th percentile, are the medians (and in these cases also generally the means). Half the people are smaller than these values, half are larger. The other points, the 1st, 5th, 95th, and 99th percentiles, tell what size *exceeds* only one percent, five percent, 95 percent, or 99 percent of the people.

The nature of the dimensions is portrayed in Figure 3.1. The various "sitting" dimensions show the distance from the seat surface the subject is sitting on, to the point named when the subject is sitting. Thus, sitting *eye* height is the distance from the seat to *eye* level. Ninety-five percent of the women have sitting eye heights of 36 inches (90 cm.) or less. To determine how high the eye height is above the floor, simply add the seat height to the sitting eye height.

In order to avoid adding variability by measuring

A table of body sizes is presented.

Table 3.1

Distribution of Body Sizes

Dimension*	Women 1%	5%	50%	95%	99%	Men 1%	5%	50%	95%	99%	Both Sexes 1%	5%	50%	95%	99%
A Weight	93(42)	104(47)	137(62)	199(91)	236(107)	112(51)	126(57)	166(76)	217(99)	241(110)	102(46)	115(52)	152(68)	208(95)	238(108)
B Standing Height	57(144)	59(149)	63(159)	67(170)	69(175)	62(157)	64(162)	68(172)	73(184)	75(190)	59(150)	62(156)	65(166)	70(177)	72(182)
C Shoulder Breadth	13(34)	14(36)	15(39)	17(44)	18(45)	15(39)	16(41)	17(44)	19(45)	20(47)	14(36)	15(38)	17(42)	17(44)	18(46)
D Chest Depth	6(15)	6(16)	7(19)	8(21)	9(22)	6(16)	7(18)	8(20)	9(23)	9(24)	6(16)	7(17)	8(20)	9(22)	9(23)
E Sitting Height	30(75)	31(78)	33(84)	36(90)	37(93)	32(81)	33(84)	36(91)	38(96)	39(99)	31(78)	32(81)	35(88)	37(93)	38(96)
F Sitting Eye Height	26(67)	27(69)	29(74)	31(79)	32(82)	28(71)	29(73)	31(78)	33(84)	34(88)	27(69)	28(71)	30(76)	32(82)	34(85)
G Sitting Shoulder Height	20(52)	21(53)	23(56)	25(60)	26(66)	21(52)	21(54)	23(59)	25(64)	26(65)	21(52)	21(54)	23(58)	24(60)	26(66)
H Sitting Elbow Height	6(16)	7(18)	9(23)	11(28)	12(30)	6(16)	7(19)	10(24)	12(29)	12(32)	6(16)	7(18)	9(24)	11(28)	12(31)
I Sitting Thigh Height	—	—	—	—	—	4(10)	5(12)	6(14)	6(16)	7(17)	—	—	—	—	—
J Elbow to Finger Tips	—	—	—	—	—	17(43)	18(45)	19(48)	20(51)	21(53)	—	—	—	—	—
K Buttocks to Front of Knee	20(51)	21(53)	22(57)	24(61)	25(63)	20(51)	21(54)	23(59)	25(64)	26(66)	20(51)	21(54)	23(58)	24(62)	25(64)
L Buttocks to Back of Knee	16(41)	17(43)	19(48)	21(53)	22(56)	16(42)	17(44)	20(50)	22(55)	23(57)	16(42)	17(44)	19(49)	21(54)	22(56)
M Floor-to Sitting Height	14(36)	15(37)	16(41)	18(44)	18(46)	15(39)	16(40)	17(43)	18(46)	19(48)	15(38)	15(38)	17(42)	18(45)	19(47)
N Upward Reach from Seat	—	—	—	—	—	—	52(130)	55(139)	59(150)	—	—	—	—	—	—
O Forward Reach from Back	28(71)	29(73)	31(79)	34(85)	34(87)	31(78)	32(81)	35(88)	37(94)	39(98)	29(74)	30(77)	33(84)	35(90)	36(92)

* Dimensions A, B, C not portrayed. Other dimensions shown in Figure 3.1. First units are inches or pounds (second units are centimeters or kilograms).

different types and amounts of clothing, most anthropometric measures are taken of nude subjects. As clothing adds only a fraction of an inch for most dimensions, it can be safely ignored by the designer.

Nudity makes little difference.

Finally, we should mention the matter of correlations among measures. Obviously, tall people tend to weigh more than short people. That is, there is *some*

Body measures are only moderately correlated.

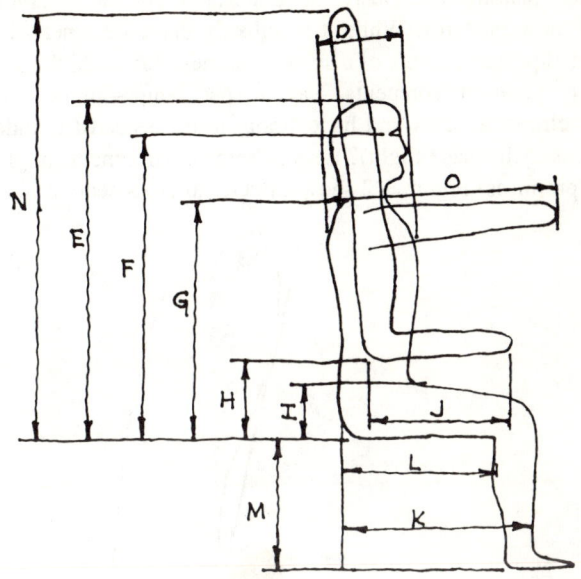

Figure 3.1 *Key to dimensions of body size.*

correlation between height and weight. But this correlation is far from perfect: many short people are heavier than many of those who are taller. This is the case for all the body measures: Their intercorrelations are not perfect. Thus, for example, one shouldn't assume that because a woman is at the 95th percentile in standing height, her reach will also be at the 95th percentile.

POSTURE

"Posture" means the arrangement of different parts, in this case of the body. An anthropologist named Hewes (1957) has discriminated 1000 postures in various cultures. Major classes include chair sitting, floor sitting, standing, nilotic standing (from the peoples of the Nile—standing with support of a pole), leaning, lying supine (on the back), lying prone (on the stomach), and squatting. Obviously, there are large cultural variations in the popularity of these postures. While it is unlikely that a designer will change the well-learned postural habits of a society, some creative thinking might be in order. In extreme environments—say, a space ship—might it not be an advantage to eliminate seats and have floor sitting instead (if, indeed, any sitting is necessary in space flight)? Less extreme environments might call for postural compromises. Figure 3.2 shows a vertical cross-section of a support

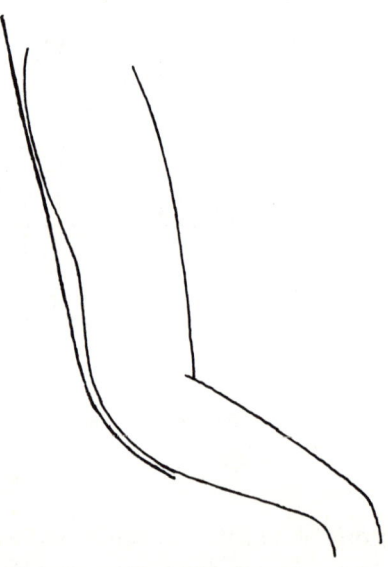

Figure 3.2 *Innovative body support.*

designed by a British designer for mass transit vehicles. This design has the advantage of taking less floor space than seats. It is also less tiring than standing because some body weight is supported by points other than the feet. This design also has the alleged advantage that it provides less exposure of miniskirt wearers.

Van Wely (1969), a Dutch industrial physician, advocates avoiding sitting for more than one hour continuously, standing for more than one half hour continuously, or for more than a total of one hour per day. This may sound ridiculous, as many jobs require violation of these rules. However, it is also true that about one third of most working groups have foot, leg, and back problems (some due to poor seating or the need to stand).

Tradition and bad judgment are responsible for many bad working postures. Redesign has enabled barbers and dentists—traditionally standing workers—to sit down. Some factory managers don't like to "coddle" their employees (Protestant work ethic) by letting them sit when generally it would be practicable. If the job requires continuous attendance at one place, then sit-standing alternation with a stool permits easy changes from sitting to standing.

SEATING

From an ergonomic standpoint, seats are the furniture of greatest importance. Many are also poorly designed. The general principle to observe in good seating is to use the maximum possible body area in support of the body. Most seating problems result from some violation of this principle.

Maximize the body area supported by a seat.

Most expensive seating is designed primarily to look good. Consider Figure 3.3. The simplicity of the

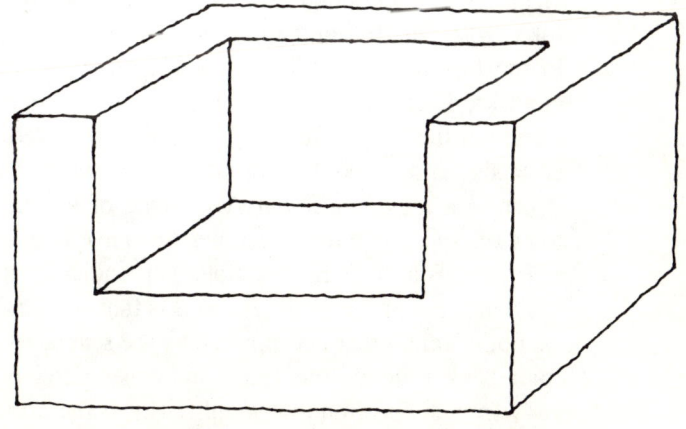

Figure 3.3 *"Cubic" chair with too-high arms.*

Visual attractiveness is an inadequate basis for design.

cube-like form is the basis for a number of attractive chairs. But, assuming a typical back height, the arms are so high (about shoulder level) that they quickly become uncomfortable. Most sitters soon place their hands in their laps. This is bad design; mere visual attractiveness is not enough.

Seat design affects all criteria.

Better design creates a seat that is comfortable for a large percentage of people. We shall give attention to this. Seat design to achieve good performance entails the relation of the seat to the rest of the workplace, and we shall take this subject up in a later section. Continued use of an uncomfortable seat and workplace can produce health problems. For example, if the sitter has to sit astraddle a large object because no knee space was provided or if a sitter either had to sit statically with his trunk twisted or had to twist it frequently, strains of medical consequence could result.

Sitting Forces

The seat back supports part of the weight.

Look at Figure 3.4! Ayoub (1971), an industrial engineer at Texas Tech University, presented this analysis. The two large L-shaped figures represent a chair. Within the chair is a diagram representing the force with which a human body presses on the chair. In the top half of the figure, a long line, A, points downward, representing a force due to gravity (the weight of the body). Such a force can be resolved, that is, analyzed or broken down into components, by constructing a rectangle about A. Instead of having one force of A size and direction, we now have two smaller forces, B and C, in directions perpendicular to the back and seat of the chair. Force B is that small part of the body weight that is supported by the seat back. The chair back relieves the spine and other parts of the body from supporting that weight. This is the principal function of the seat back.

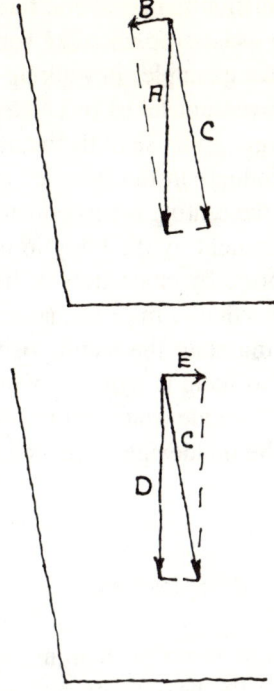

Figure 3.4 *Analysis of sitting forces.*

Force C, perpendicular to B, shows what weight is left to be held up after back support is provided. Force C is analyzed in the lower half of Figure 3.4. A vertical force D is that largest part of body weight that is supported through the buttocks and possibly the thighs by the seat base. Force E is what is left over. Its thrust is in the direction of forcing the sitter out of the seat. To counter it requires a small resisting force exerted by the sitter through his legs and feet unless the seat base is tilted upward to provide resistance. To make a seat uncomfortable (as is apparently done in some "quickie" eating places to produce customer turnover), one would tilt the seat base downward to increase force E and the sitter would tire more quickly resisting it.

Most of the weight is supported by the buttocks.

Much static work results from seat misdesign.

Much difficulty in seat comfort results from *static work*. In the usual *dynamic work* some part of the body is moving, for example, in walking or lifting. In static work no movement takes place. Such work leads to physical fatigue because of the inadequate exchange of chemical products in the muscles and elsewhere. For example, if the seating is inadequate the lower arms or back must be held by the body in position rather than being supported by chair arms or back. Static work is stressful to particular muscles, as certain muscles must contract to maintain the static position. Although we design jobs to include dynamic work tasks, we rarely deliberately include static work. Static work is the product of the maldesign of seats and other aspects of the workplace.

Design Do's and Don'ts

There is no one healthy posture.

1. There is no such thing as *the one* healthy posture. Usually heavy physical work is done in a standing position. If the worker is seated, heavy work is best done without a back rest. Extensive arm movements preclude arm rests.

The trunk should be nearly upright.

2. For work seating (and most leisure seating as well) the trunk should be supported in a more-or-less upright position. Figure 3.5 shows results of unpublished research on the preferred seat back angle. College students who had just performed a visual task were asked to judge how well they would like to perform the task for eight hours a day with their chair backs in particular positions. A clear preference is found for 15° (or 105°, reading from the horizontal). It is interesting that the supine position is the poorest of those studied. Evidently, college students don't want to lie down on the job.

Support the back up to the shoulder blades.

3. Much writing on seat design emphasizes support of the small of the back. Indeed, most back

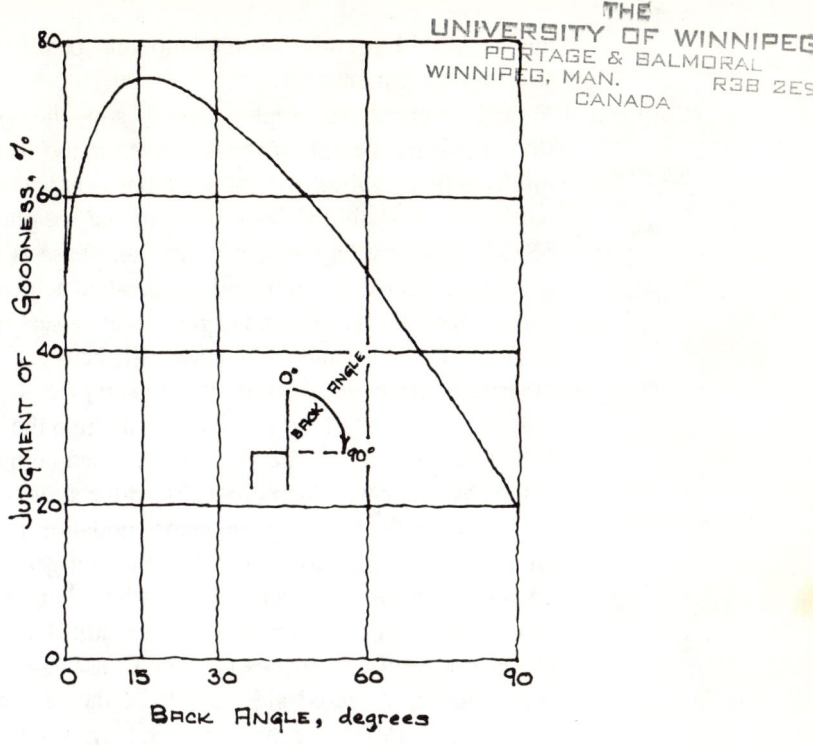

Figure 3.5 Goodness of seat back angles.

complaints deal with this region. Better seat back support extends upward to the shoulder blades. The back rest should never be absent for people over 30 years of age.

4. Movement should be possible to enable shifting of the body parts that are supporting the weight, thus maximizing body area contact. The seat should not be highly contoured to fit the body, for that will restrict movement. *Seats should permit movement.*

5. Upholstery increases the area of the body that supports the weight and is desirable for that reason. Upholstery should have limited compressibility. Heavy pressure through the hand should depress the padding only an inch or so. If padding is too soft *Some upholstery is desirable.*

the body will become locked into one position, restricting movement.

Proper seat base height is important.

6. Seat base height should suit the sitter's floor-to-sitting height. If the seat base is too low, the thighs will be raised off the seat base, and the buttocks, which should support most of the weight, will be only partially on the seat. If the seat base is much too low it places the trunk and thighs at an acute angle and compresses the internal organs. Such a seat is also difficult to get on and off for the tall, heavy, old, or otherwise disabled. This problem is typical of auto seating. However, if the seat base is too high the lower legs will "dangle" at the knees rather than being supported by the feet, which produces undue stress on the underside of the thighs. One accommodation is to sit on the front edge of the seat base, thus not getting the advantage of the seat back. The seat base height measured at the seat reference point in non-adjustable seating is frequently 18 inches (46 cm.) (The *seat reference point* is centered side-to-side at the rear of the seat base.). Reference to Table 3.1 shows that 18 inches exceeds floor-to-sitting height not only for 99 percent of women but also 95 percent of men. This "standard" height is simply too high. This height is a compromise meant to fit desk and table heights, which are also too high. More on this later. An adjustable seat base height, ranging from 15 inches (37 cm.) to 18 inches (45 cm.), is a good solution, though usually expensive. (Can you think of an inexpensive solution?) Most adjustable features of chairs are wasted either because they are never adjusted or because they are not adjusted properly. A generally cheaper solution is to have non-adjustable seats of varying seat base heights to match with the sitter. A third solution is to make the seat base too high but to provide a foot rest. In any case there is the need to match seat base height to the individual.

Seat bases should be the proper depth.

7. The seat base depth or length must also be a

proper size. If the seat base is too short, the weight will be supported by an inadequate portion of the buttocks and thighs. If the seat base is too long it will place pressure on the back side of the calves. Again, as with the too-high seat base, an accommodation to the too-long seat base is to sit forward on the seat, thus not benefitting from the seat back.

Cheaper work seats and stools generally have too-short seat bases. Leisure seating frequently has too-long seat bases. The latter may be slightly tempered by the presence of upholstery. The buttocks-to-back-of-knee length from the 5th percentile woman to the 95th percentile man varies from 21 inches (53 cm.) to 24 inches (62 cm.) (Table 3.1). A simple design solution is to make seat depth slightly shorter than necessary for the 5th percentile woman. This seat will not be so short as to create great difficulty for the 95th percentile man.

8. Generally, arm rests should be provided. These may be attached to the chair at a height that places the forearms more-or-less horizontal. As may be seen in Table 3.1, the 5th percentile woman's elbow height is only 7 inches while the 95th percentile man's is 12 inches above the seat base. Adjustability or multiple seat sizes would cope with this wide range. In many cases the work surface, a desk or bench top, especially if padded, would substitute for seat-mounted arm rests. *Arm rests are needed.*

9. If seat height is too great to permit resting the feet flat on the floor, a foot rest should be provided, as with the too-high chair or the stool. The foot rest should measure at least 2 feet by 2 feet to permit change of position of the feet. Most stool foot rests are quite inadequate. *Foot rests may be needed.*

10. Stools are sensible seats when the user is confined to one spot, enabling him to sit or stand readily. Stools are almost always poorly designed for seat comfort, however. For example, stools should *For some jobs stools are desirable.*

have back rests. The stool is frequently selected rather than a chair to keep lower-status workers "in their place" and because it is cheap.

Measuring Seat Comfort

Seat comfort is determined by sitting.

Much seat comfort research has been done, but the comfort of any newly designed seat should be evaluated. The prime consideration is actually to measure seat comfort by sitting and judging rather than to judge by looking at the seat. Two reports bear this out. Kroemer (1968) surveyed seat dimensions recommended by a number of European "experts." For example, recommended seat base height varied from fourteen to 23 inches (35 to 59 cm.). Only a basketball center would fit a 23-inch seat base height. In another case, Shackel and his colleagues (1969) studied the long-term (in hours) seat comfort of ten armless, "straight-back" chairs. Then they had eight ergonomic seating "experts" rate the chairs. The comfort rankings of only one of the eight experts showed any correlation with the comfort test results, and that correlation was quite modest. However, as Wachsler and Learner (1960) showed, people's ratings of seat comfort after five minutes of sitting correlated very highly with their ratings after four hours. This is true even though the comfort rating of any seat will decline over time.

Although seat comfort research results can be used to predict seat comfort, once the seat is designed or selected it should be tested for comfort. The March 1969 issue of *Ergonomics* is the best single collection of seat comfort research available.

THE WORKPLACE

Work place design is critical for performance.

Seat design is primarily a problem in maintaining comfort, but in the design of the rest of the workplace, performance plays a major role. Generally, we want to design a workplace that will provide for detailed visual tasks and for use of the fingers, hands, and arms. There are considerations of both vision and static work.

Seeing Detail

If one is trying to distinguish very small detail visually, then moving it closer to the eyes will make the detail seem larger. The reason is that the number of degrees or fractions of a degree that the detail subtends or extends over the retina (sensing portion) of the eye will be larger. Thus, the actual physical area of the retina that is stimulated is larger as the detail is moved closer; and one will be able to perceive the detail. There is a limit, however, to how close something can be to the eyes and still be seen clearly. This limit is called the *near point*. (Determine your own near point. Without your glasses move some printed matter close to your eyes until you find the closest point where you can read it easily.) For children the near point is just a few inches from the eyes. As we get older, the near point slowly moves farther from the eyes. Around 40 years of age a sharp change takes place, and the near point moves more rapidly away from the eyes. Figure 3.6 shows these changes. What happens is that with age the lens of the eye hardens and is more difficult to shape. Further, the ciliary muscles that control the shape of the lens during accommodation become less effective; they are less able to squeeze the lens to make it thicker to allow seeing at close distance. The near point defines the limit on close seeing for brief periods. For longer periods of time, seeing at the near point is uncomfortable. One rule of thumb is, for an 8-hour job, seeing distance should be at least twice the near point.

The near point limits closeness of viewing.

Some unpublished research of the author is

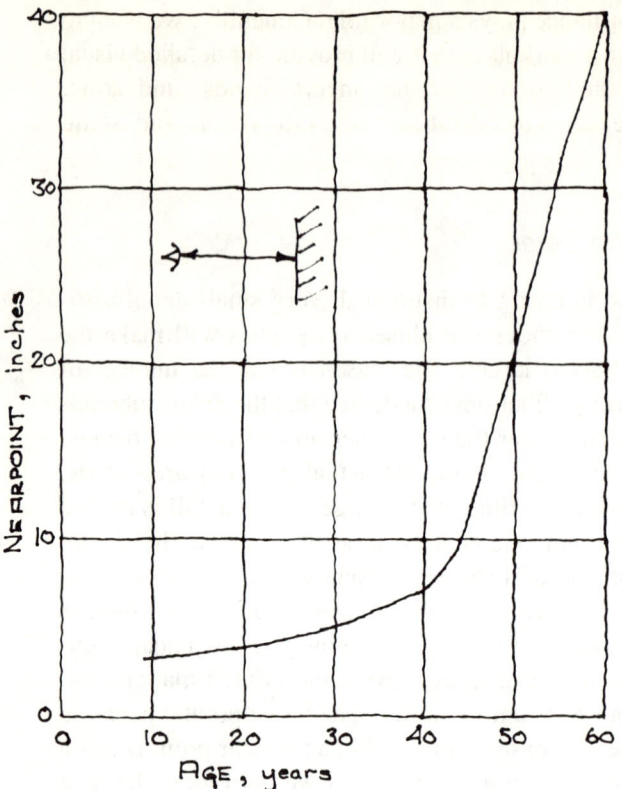

Figure 3.6 Nearpoint with age.

For difficult seeing put the task close.

shown in Figure 3.7. First, college students performed a visual-acuity task to determine their thresholds for visual detail, that is, what size detail they could see about half the time. In other words, this was a small and difficult task. These threshold tasks were then shown to them at various distances. They were asked to judge, "If you were required to perform this task for eight hours a day, how satisfactory would you find this viewing condition?" The center curve, "Threshold Task," shows these results. When the display was about twice the subjects' near point, the subjects rated the viewing distance best and as the viewing distance was increased out to a meter, the viewing distance was deemed to be poorer and poorer until worthless. Obviously, with this difficult visual task, people preferred to look closely. Because of the nature of the experimental set-up, this desire to be close is partly an effect of the task actually being larger when it is close, partly it must have been due to some other effect. Undoubtedly the subjects underestimated the discomfort they would incur in extended-time seeing when judging it during these brief viewings at the near distances.

The lowest curve in Figure 3.7, "Below-

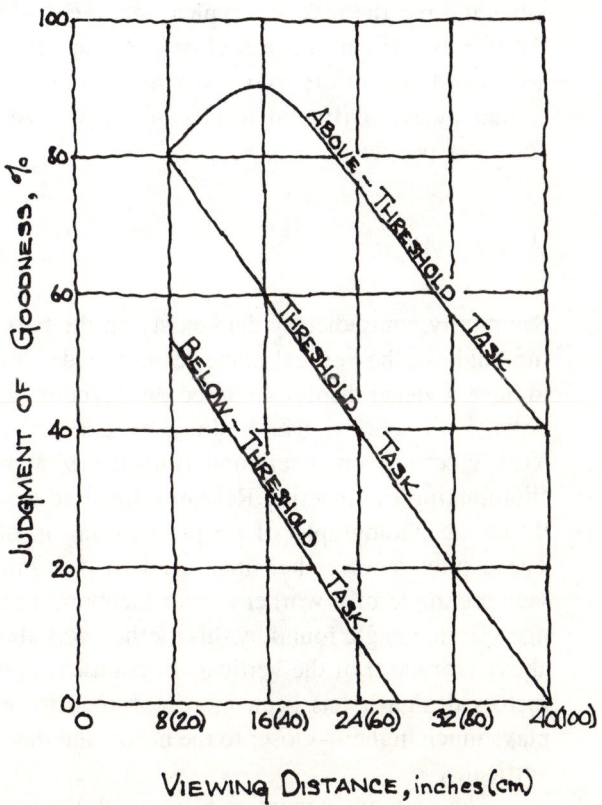

Figure 3.7 *Goodness of viewing distance with size of task.*

There is no good distance for very difficult tasks.

Threshold Task," represents similar data to that of the Threshold Task. Here smaller detail (less frequently seen correctly) was used in judging viewing distance. Again, the closest distance tested was judged the best viewing distance. Judged goodness dropped steadily with increased viewing to zero at about 28 inches, which was sometimes considered a magic viewing distance for above-threshold tasks.

For easy seeing, 15 inches is an optimum.

The third task involved detail distinctly above the threshold level—detail typical of reading or the usual work task. Here an optimal viewing distance was found at 15 inches, a common reading distance.

Keep detail large.

The moral is keep the task detail as large as possible and put the task at a typical reading distance. If the task is difficult move it closer. Perhaps if the task were even easier (larger) one would want to position it farther away. (Different results might well be found for older people.)

Viewing Angle

There is some confusion about the best vertical viewing angle.

Seemingly contradictory data exists on the best viewing angle in the vertical plane. Side-to-side, it is best to have a visual display centered on the body. Up and down isn't so obvious. A study by Crouch, a New York electrical engineer, and Buttolf (1973) for the Illuminating Engineering Research Institute was done by taking photographs of people working in offices. These photos were then measured to determine the viewing angle of a worker at that location. The average viewing angle found by this method was about 25° above (forward) of the vertical. In contrast, in human factors design it has been more common to put displays much higher—closer to the horizontal than to the vertical.

The previously mentioned research by the author on back angle and viewing distance also studied the vertical viewing angle. The visual display was varied above and below the horizontal (defined here as perpendicular to the back angle). Students judged the satisfactoriness of the viewing angle for visual work over 8 hours. Figure 3.8 shows the results. Positions

Best angles are perpendicular to, or below the back angle.

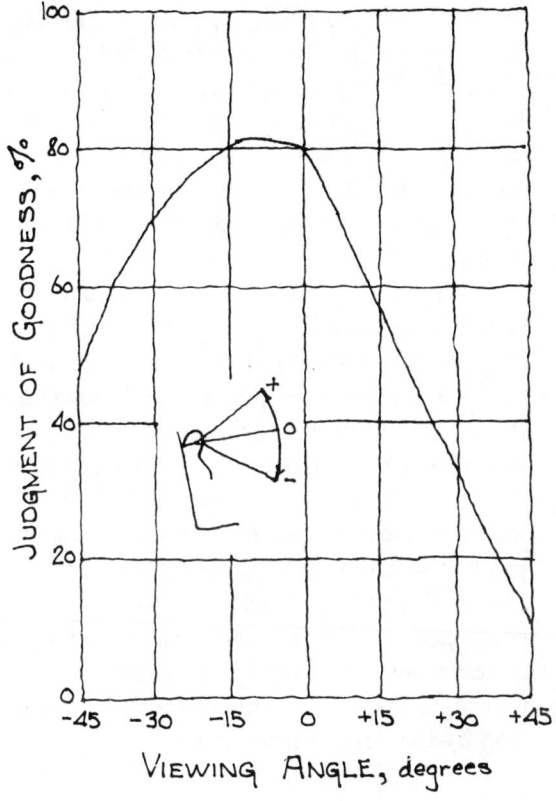

Figure 3.8 *Goodness of viewing angle.*

from 0° to 15° below the horizontal were deemed the best viewing angles. As viewing went above the horizontal, it rapidly was judged poorer. This is the "front pew" effect: It has been frequently noted how churchgoers avoid the front pews. Although some have interpreted this phenomenon as avoidance of a close confrontation with God's representative, it is more likely caused by the discomfort suffered when looking upward. The muscles in the back of the neck are compressed when the head is tilted backward.

People frequently are looking down.

The more common downward looking may be seen by observing people walking or standing around. Generally, their heads are untilted or tilted downward. One design implication concerns the location of signs. Signs are frequently placed high in a room or on a building or pole where they are less likely to be obscured by furniture and other people. However, such signs may not even be noticed by people wanting their information.

At desks the hands determine looking.

Why did the office study show such different results? People in offices are usually reading or writing on materials on their desks. Here the limitation is primarily one of hand position and viewing distance. If the elbows were positioned at one's sides with forearms held horizontally, the viewing angle would be about 40° above the vertical. If work were done with the elbows drawn back, then to look at the hand position would be to look closer to the vertical, say 25° above it. Further, if materials on a desk could be positioned at 15° below the horizontal, they would be quite far away. In typing or reading or writing, the viewing angle is determined more by work location than by the desired head angle.

Hand Activities

Primary hand height is at elbow height.

The primary area for hand and finger activities is about a foot and a half wide, centered side-to-side, at elbow height or somewhat lower, and centered within 4 inches to either side of a line about 10 inches in front of the body. Frequent operations or critical operations should be located here. A secondary hand activity extends from the back of the primary area up and away to shoulder height at an extended arm's distance of about 28 inches. The secondary nature of this area can be appreciated by picturing a typewriter keyboard within it. Tertiary work areas can be defined in areas other than these. Such areas can be used for unimportant and infrequent operations. Woodson (1972), a San Diego human-factors specialist, gives more details on such matters.

For the primary and secondary areas, the surfaces so defined are for hands. If tools or equipment such as a keyboard are to be used, the table or work surface should be lower to accommodate these implements. Figure 3.9 shows a woman seated at a keyboard inap-

Tool use may require lower work surfaces.

Figure 3.9 *Too-high hand area; too-far display.*

propriately located closer to breast height than to elbow height. Note also the excessive viewing distance (about 26 inches) in this ill-conceived advertising photo.

Standard desk/table heights are too high.

One of the poorest workplace "standards" is the usual desk or table height of 29 or 30 inches. Consider three cases from Table 3.1, the 50th percentile of both sexes, the 5th percentile of women, and the 95th percentile of men. The floor-to-sitting heights for these three cases respectively are:

17 inches (42 cm.) 15 inches (37 cm.) 18 inches (46 cm.).

We would like to sit people of these sizes on seats of these heights. The sitting elbow heights for these cases are:

9 inches (24 cm.) 7 inches (18 cm.) 12 inches (29 cm.).

These are the maximum desired work surface heights above the seat. Adding, to find the desirable height above the floor, we get:

26 inches (66 cm.) 22 inches (55 cm.) 30 inches (75 cm.).

(Except for the 50th percentile, this process of adding leads to slight errors due to "regression toward the mean" effects caused by the lack of perfect correlation between the two measures.) Only the 95th percentile man is suited for a 30-inch work surface. For the average man and woman the desk or table is 4 inches too high—much too high. For the small woman it is 8 inches too high—ridiculously so. If such a work surface height must be used, the seat height should be raised to attain a sitting elbow height of 7 to 12 inches (18 to 29 cm.). This means a seat height of 23 to 18 inches (58 to 46 cm.). Except for the large man, a footrest will be needed.

A stool height of 30 inches is frequently satisfactory.

If a sit-stand posture using a stool or a standing-only posture is adopted, the same relationship between the work-surface height and the sitting-elbow height should be maintained. As we frequently wish to have the same work surface suitable for standing or stool sitting we need to set the work surface for standing and adjust the stool height.

Standing elbow height data are not directly available, but they can be calculated. Standing shoulder heights (not in Table 3.1) for the 50th percentile of both sexes, the 5th percentile of women, and the 95th percentile of men are:

54 inches (137 cm.)   48 inches (122 cm.)
60 inches (152 cm.).

Shoulder to elbow length (not tabled) for the same cases are:

14 inches (36 cm.)   12 inches (30 cm.)
16 inches (40 cm.).

Subtracting to estimate standing elbow height gives:

40 inches (101 cm.)   36 inches (92 cm.)
44 inches (112 cm.).

The work surface height should be set accordingly. Then subtracting sitting elbow height estimates stool heights as:

31 inches (77 cm.)   29 inches (74 cm.)
32 inches (83 cm.).

These dimensions are fairly close to a common stool height of 30 inches.

A disadvantage of this height is that the body's center of gravity while seated on the stool is several inches higher than when standing so that some effort is required in getting on and off the stool. Perhaps the most important point to be made about stools is that

Stools should be elevated chairs, with footrests.

they should be elevated chairs—with well-designed seats, back and arm rests, and foot rests large enough to permit foot movements. These are rare qualities in stools. Many seated positions that use stools could well be redesigned to use chairs. The same is true of standing. Most standing work positions could be seated, but tradition advocates standing.

HARDWARE

Ergonomics also applies to hardware.

Woodson has treated hardware aspects of interior space design in some detail. Here we mean such things as handles for doors, windows, and drawers and plumbing, lighting, heating, and cooling fixtures and controls. A principle for the designer to remember is that the various design criteria all apply—hardware should be safe, readily operated, comfortable when used, and good-looking. Too often the space designer either ignores the selection of hardware completely—perhaps leaving it to a sub-contractor—or considers only the aesthetics.

The interior designer should consider human use of hardware.

In designing or selecting for safe, efficient, and comfortable operation, the designer needs to consider location, size, and force requirements in terms of the human user. Generally, it is not necessary to involve esoteric principles of design or tables of anthropometric data. The designer must be concerned, think through how the hardware will be used, and test it. Consider such straightforward ideas as putting a door handle on the opening side of a door instead of in the middle or making a handle fit the hand—not too large or small or ornate, not requiring too much force for many people. Two minor but frequently important considerations are making the hardware look like what it is (rather than disguising it) and designing so that fingerprints will not end up all over the surface. Servicing should be considered, for instance, in changing bulbs. In one type of space, the bathroom, Kira (1976), a Cornell architect, has done a magnificent job of analyzing the hardware requirements. Woodson (1976) has summarized many hardware needs in Table 3.2.

Table 3.2

Common Hardware Problem Areas

Windows

- Ease of opening, closing, locking, unlocking
- Ease of cleaning both sides
- Ease of seeing that the window is closed so that people do not walk through, push furniture through, or fall through
- Ease of use as an emergency escape route

Doors

- Ease of opening, closing, locking, unlocking
- Clearance for both people and furnishings
- Weather-proof
- Nonsticking, nonrattling
- Soundproof
- Fireproof
- Ventilation through
- Seeing that sliding glass door is closed so that people do not walk through
- Clearance around in order to get past or get wheelchair into room
- Emergency door hardware operable by weakest from a wheelchair
- Opens with, not against traffic flow
- Door locations to east traffic flow, expedite emergency escape, control noise

Stairs

- Optimize for user(s), not for leftover space
- Accessible for both people and furnishings
- Handrails to fit both children and adults, to prevent children from falling through or getting stuck in
- Minimize number of continuous steps to conserve energy and minimize stress
- Have ramps for wheelchairs

Hallways

- Passage to fit capacity (furniture as well as people)
- Straight, not curved or changing pathway (consider rush, bottlenecks, intersections)
- Signs, markings to help one find his way
- Illuminate
- No large fillets at base of wall that people might step on
- No slick floors
- No visual glare at ends of hallway

Cabinetry

- Design to fit articles to be stored, not just to fit leftover space
- Drawer slides for heavy loads—provide stops
- Watch for door-fold interference, drawer clearance
- Handles that fit, not just pretty or absent or camouflaged
- Doors that stay open or closed
- Locks on critical doors or drawers
- Avoid deep inaccessible cupboards or drawers

Plumbing / Fixtures

- Splash
- Bumping head
- Handles that fit, operate logically, easily, accurately
- Contact hazard removal
- Handrails, handholds
- Nonslick surfaces
- Accessible for repair
- Do not produce noise, vibration
- Consider potential leak problems

Built-in Light Fixtures / Switches

- Right location (illuminate task, not observer)
- Access for relamping, cleaning
- Optimize light distribution (minimize shadow, glare)
- Locate switches so they can be found, reached

Electrical Conveniences

- Adequate number, located where needed
- Accessible not only to normal adults but also to children, wheelchair operator
- Make childproof

- Make shockproof

Heating / Cooling System & Equipment

- Ventilation not degraded when doors are closed
- Continued ventilation when power fails
- Understandable controls
- Automatic sensors(s) located where they sense the pertinent conditions
- Locate vents for optimum performance, not ease of installation
- Vents that can be controlled (reliable, do not break off or not close completely)
- Watch out for noise produced by system or that passes through system

Storage

- Space should fit purpose
- Space should be convenient, accessible
- Space should be illuminated
- Consider fire, explosion hazards
- Consider closure requirements (ease of, locking, interference)
- Storage fixtures, shelving to fit

Most Common User-Interface Failure Points

- People have to locate themselves with respect to parking, building, entrance, interior hallway, doors, spaces.
- People have to see where they are going (illumination).
- People have to manipulate—doors, windows, drawers, faucets, thermostats, etc.
- People have to see signs, printed matter, written material, instrument faces, etc. (color, brightness, contrast, format, illumination).
- People have to maintain balance and posture control, have help to move (handholds, handrails).
- People have to move themselves or furnishings about—clearance (doors, hallways, stairs); stairs.
- People have to clean, replace, refurbish, repair.
- People need to store things.
- People may have to escape in a hurry—routes, more than one exit, emergency illumination, etc.
- People need peace and quiet, also need to have their fun without bothering others.
- People need power conveniences for their electrical add-ons, tools, hobbies, etc.
- People need reasonable thermal environment and good ventilation.

DISCUSSION

Consider a variety of work and play positions, for example, school teacher, sports spectator, assembly-line worker, kitchen worker, television watcher. Why are these performed in their usual postures with or without their usual seats? What alternative postures and seats might be considered?

MUSICAL CHAIRS

For the evaluation of chairs, explore the relation, if any, between the visual appearance and the seating comfort of chairs.

Divide the group into pairs. Have as many chairs as pairs. If there are 20 in the group, you might have two sets of five chairs.

Although any type of seat may be used, or even standing, it may be best to restrict the seats to one class, such as non-adjustable, armless, straight-backed chairs. A variety of the class of seats should be included, for example, a traditional wooden school chair, a padded contemporary chair, and an office chair.

Blindfold one member of each pair. Then have the other member lead the blindfolded member to the chairs. The blindfolded member is seated in one chair. The other member judges its visual appearance and apparent comfort on the scale that follows. The blindfold member is asked to make any comments she has on the seating comfort. ("The back hits me in the wrong place.") At the end of five minutes she judges its comfort. Use the following scale for all judgments:

1	2	3	4	5
very poor	poor	fair	good	very good

Pairs then change chairs until all chairs have been assessed. Write brief descriptions and make measurements of the chairs, or provide these.

Write a report presenting all the data, an analysis of the seat features in relation to comfort, and whether "we should buy this seat." Could this sitting test be used for actual design jobs?

REFERENCES

AYOUB, M. M. *Posture in industry*. Paper presented at meeting of the Human Factors Society, New York City, October 1971.

BROOKES, M. Biomechanics of outside female telephone workers. Talk given at Kansas State University, May 1975.

CROUCH, C. L., and L. J. BUTTOLPH. Visual relationships in office tasks. *Lighting Design and Application,* 3(5):23-25, 1973.

HERTZBERG, H. T. E. Engineering anthropology. In H. P. VAN COTT, and R. G. KINKADE (eds.). *Human engineering guide to equipment design.* (rev. ed.), Washington: U.S. Government Printing Office, 1972.

HEWES, G. W. The anthropology of posture. *Scientific American,* 196(2):122-132, 1957.

KIRA, B. *The bathroom.* (2nd ed.) New York: Viking Press, 1976.

KROEMER, K. H. E., and J. C. ROBINETTE. *Ergonomics in the design of office furniture.* Wright Patterson AFB, Ohio: Aeromedical Research Laboratory, 1968. AMRL-TR-68-80.

OXFORD, H. W. Anthropometric data for educational chairs. *Ergonomics,* 12(2):140-161, 1969.

SHACKEL, B., K. D. CHIDSEY, and P. SHIPLEY. The assessment of chair comfort, *Ergonomics,* 12(2): 269-306, 1969.

VAN WELY, P. *Design and disease.* Manhattan, Kansas: Kansas Engineering Experiment Station, 1969 (Special Report 86).

WACHSLER, R. A., and D. B. LEARNER. An analysis of some factors influencing seat comfort. *Ergonomics,* 3(4):315-320, 1960.

WOODSON, W. E. Design of individual workplaces. In H. P. VAN COTT, and R. G. KINKADE. *Human engineering guide to equipment design.* Washington: U. S. Government Printing Office, 1972.

WOODSON, W. E. Human factors engineering on architectural hardware. *Environmental Design News,* 7(3), 1976.

Smaller Spaces

"Be close to your fellow man, but not too close."

The design of small spaces that involve only a few people should be based to a great extent on social-motivational factors. In spaces of short-term occupancy such as waiting rooms people may or may not wish to socialize. Conversation is facilitated by having people face toward each other. How close physically people want to be to each other depends on the closeness of their social relationship. In spaces of long-term occupancy such as offices, personalizing of one's territory is commonplace and should be explicitly considered by the designer. Again, the furniture arrangements, such as barriers, will influence people's reactions to the space.

Design to meet the objectives of the space.

Whatever the size or type of the space, interior space design begins with the objectives for the space, aiming at the satisfaction of the activities to be carried out there. In a place of work it includes the satisfactory performance of work tasks. In a living room or bedroom it probably means satisfying the relaxing and socializing activities. In the previous chapter we dealt with the individual's workplace and its furnishings. In that case anthropometric considerations dominate design. In the next chapter, dealing with spaces for many people and things, arrangement to minimize the movements of people and materials dominates design. In the present case we are concerned with the design of spaces for a relatively small number of people—some offices and waiting rooms, for example. These include homogeneous spaces like large restaurants that involve many repetitions of smaller space units. Here individuals' social motivations are most important.

ANIMAL CONCEPTS

Ethologists devote considerable effort to observing various animal species in their natural habitats in order to see what happens. Experimental psychologists sometimes create specialized environments for animals, to try to determine the influence of various environmental characteristics. Concepts and relationships useful in explaining these animal behaviors may be useful in thinking about human behavior. Generally, these are merely *analogous* uses of terms because subhuman animal behavior is much more dominated by instinctive actions than is human behavior. It is not even certain that there are any human instinctive behaviors, although there are unlearned reflexes in humans that may keep us alive long enough to learn adaptive behavior which continues to protect us.

Territoriality is an animal concept that has a central usefulness in interior space design. In a variety of vertebrate species, the male animals mark off an area or territory for themselves and members of their social group. They may defend this territory from others—protecting their food supply or mates or what have you. Male dogs, for example, spend considerable time marking off prominent landmarks in the neighborhood such as fireplugs, tall weeds, and auto wheels by urinating on them. In many species this territoriality behavior may have survival value by providing some population control or guarding against *overcrowding*. If an intruder makes a *spatial invasion* of an animal's territory, the animal in its own territory has a relative advantage in competing because of its home territory's familiarity and importance. Experiments have been conducted on rats or other species where the animals live in very

...ions. The crowded populations go through various phases, ... high death rates. Notable with crowding is that many or ... velop aberrant behavior, especially in how they relate to ... their sexual relations. As Lawrence (1974) has pointed ... animal experimentation is of little direct value to man.

TEMPORARY OCCUPANCY

Determine the social object of the space.

Here we are concerned with spaces like waiting rooms where the occupancy tends to be brief. A distinction among spaces and intentions for spaces needs to be made, as we're not always trying to accomplish the same end. The space may be intended to facilitate either social behavior or individual behavior. Generally, in libraries, public transit, waiting rooms, and cafeterias the objective should be to foster isolation of the individual or the existing small group from others. The individual is here to study, to get to Manhattan, to wait with her mother for the dentist, or to eat with her male friend. For the most part there is no desire to socialize with others, although on rare occasions a conversation may be struck up. The need is for what has been called a *sociofugal space*—one which leads away from social activity. The contrary situation is true in livingrooms, many drinking places, and a few eating places. In the latter case, normally sociofugal places such as restaurants should be *sociopetal,* that is, seeking to foster sociability, where the clientele is a relatively small closed group, as in a city neighborhood, a small town, or a campus. Here we want to facilitate social contact.

Desired seating arrangements depend on social relations.

A lot of research has been done on how people sit in relation to one another when they do or don't want to socialize. Sommer (1967), a California psychologist, and Knapp (1972), a Purdue psychologist, have summarized much of this and related work. Although the results don't seem altogether consistent, one can derive a few conclusions. If people are intimate friends and want to talk and snuggle they will most likely want to sit side by side, preferably on a sofa or loveseat, only inches apart. If the relationship is less friendly such proximity is not desired, and sofas should rarely be used. If friendly but not intimate socializing is desired for talking and looking, a face-to-face seating (or perhaps a 90-degree facing) is desired, at most a few feet apart. An intervening table, particularly a low one, does not constitute an intolerable barrier. A less than best arrangement for friendly talkers is side-by-side seating. Direction and distance are critical.

Hall (1959) has stated distances that he believes are desirable distances for conversing by people in various relationships. These include: intimate, less than 18 inches; "casual" (friendly), 2½ to 4 feet; and "social-consultation" (formal), 7 to 12 feet. The author once had an office arranged with a chair positioned on his side of the desk for a visitor about 3 feet from him. Invariably, visiting students would shove the chair back against the wall another 3 feet away. As these distances are culturally determined, people from some other societies prefer closer conversing distances than Americans. I once met a friend, a professor from Southern Europe, in the student union lobby, and we began to talk. My acquaintance stood very close to me; I backed away. He moved closer; I backed away. We moved a fair distance across the lobby before I realized what was happening and quit backing off.

Desired distances depend on the people.

Sommer (1969) reports some results on social group size in public places. Because even in sociofugal places we want to provide for the existing group, there may be implications for furniture selection and arrangements. This study found that over 70 percent of the groups were of only two people!

Most public social groups are small.

Twenty-one percent had three people, 6 percent four people, and only 2 percent had five or more people. That the smallness of social group size has generally been ignored by designers is evident in the large number of table and seat groupings for four and more people in restaurants and waiting areas. The result is waste space with one or two people occupying spaces meant for larger groups.

People want to face activity.

Another frequently discussed concept is *defensive seating*. It has been observed that people will frequently select chairs in public places facing outward with their backs to the wall. Comparison has been made to the back-to-the-wall sitting in western movies where the sitter wants to avoid being shot in the back. In contemporary life, being shot in the back is a low-probability event. What people are doing is not protecting their backs but facing the music (action). A study of a company cafeteria by Flynn (1973), a Pennsylvania State architect, and his Kent State colleagues demonstrates this: Employees came individually or in small groups into the cafeteria. They sat at round tables. There was one public entrance to the room at the foot of a stairway, where newcomers entered. As places at the tables filled up, the chairs facing the entrance were filled first, then the adjacent seats, and finally the seats facing away from the entrance. Later, the wall opposite the entrance on which some large murals were located was lighted so that the murals became something to see. Now the tendency was for people to sit facing the murals rather than the entrance!

Seat arrangements can be selected.

If the designer wants to facilitate sociability, she places the right number of seats to face each other at appropriate distances. In the nonsocial spaces the designer does the opposite. She has people who don't care to socialize sit facing the same direction or away from each other, such as outward around a pillar or back to back. Whatever the facing relationship, she can place seats far apart—the farther the better. The person wishing *privacy* rather than sociability can help himself: The student wishing to study in the cafeteria goes into the corner and faces the wall. The person wishing to avoid contact in the waiting room puts his coat down on the sofa beside him. (How many times have you seen a sofa in a waiting room fully occupied by sitters? Or in a living room? Answer: only when all other spaces were used or if other seating was even more awkward.)

In some cases the designer doesn't realize what she should try to accomplish or how. Sommer (1969) gives the example of a sitting area in a mental institution. One way of describing most mental patients is that they have developed generally unsatisfactory social graces. They need to learn how to relate to other people better. In the mental institution, unless we merely want to care for the patients forever, we need to help them learn to relate to people better. In the sitting room, Sommer observed the most extreme sociofugal seating—chairs lined up along the walls at considerable distances apart and around the pillars. Hardly anyone was facing at a conversational distance. This was apparently done to facilitate maintenance and other service functions, surely placing the cart before the horse. Chairs in living rooms are frequently placed along the walls, too far apart, with little thought for consequences. The typical living room is an awkward size. Living rooms (like school class sizes) should be made smaller to obtain greater intimacy or larger to accommodate several small conversational groups.

Some design ignores social needs.

Kleeman (1975), a Midwestern interior designer and ergonomist, tried to facilitate interpersonal activity in a mental ward and was able to double it. Working with patients' participation, various activity areas were developed where people could meet. For this type of person it was important to have sociopetal spaces where people could easily get in and out of the

Interpersonal activity can be fostered.

group and where—with partial barriers—they could partially join the group, until self-assurance developed.

LONG-TERM OCCUPANCY

Personalization is important in private spaces.

In less-public spaces like offices, bedrooms, and livingrooms, the occupant tends to have a long-term association with the space—my living room, my desk, my room—and territoriality takes on new significance. The occupant is inclined to personalize the space, that is, to decorate it with materials that are somewhat distinctive—his diploma, his pot of violets, his centerfold photo.

Institutions provide rather barren spaces.

Although the space-providing organization ("the management") frequently gets upset at these graffiti, they are both inevitable and desirable. Inevitability stems from the stark nature of the spaces provided to the occupant. If the institution provides the office-holder a desk, a chair, a file cabinet, a bookcase, a light in the ceiling, and tile on the floor, it generally feels it has done very well. As each such space is probably like every other such space in the building, the occupant will usually want to mark off his space as his and sometimes try to beautify it. For instance, in a study by the author of 30 private and semiprivate faculty offices, all but four had put some kind of material—artistic or academic—on the office wall. However, only a few had carpeted or put plants or drapes or curtains into their offices.

User beautification may seem tasteless.

Indeed, to the designer when "beautification" does take place it is frequently considered tasteless and ruinous to the overall design effect. There have even been cases where designers returned in later months to order personalizations removed. One famous architect of an Eastern state university campus placed a clause in his contract that the university would not allow any posters on campus, in order not to spoil the effect of his design.

Personalization is desirable, however, not only because of the immediate satisfaction it provides the occupant but also because of the increased sense of identification with the employing institution ("In my office at the bank, I have a picture of the smog over Chicago."). Where possible the designer should foster more and better personalization. If the prospective occupant is available during design, it should be possible to ascertain his tastes and to have him participate in incorporating them into the design or making provision for them—a special wall for pictures, for example—or even to improve the occupant's tastes. Such design constraints must be looked at as opportunities for designer creativity, rather than as nuisances.

Personalization is desirable.

An arrangement issue that often arises in offices and to lesser extent in other spaces such as classrooms is the use of barriers. In the left part of Figure 4.1 is

Barriers are sometimes created.

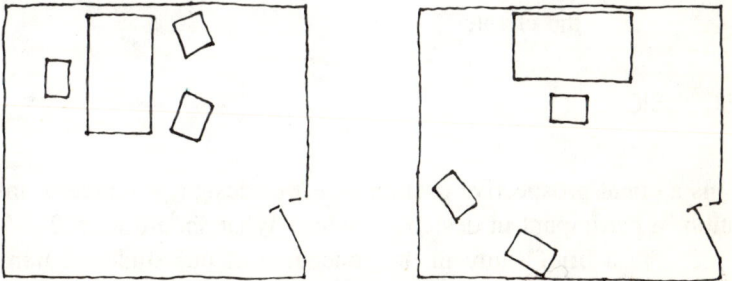

Figure 4.1 Offices with and without a barrier.

shown a common private office arrangement. It enables the occupant to face the music and it keeps the visitors, whom the occupant may be uneasy about, separated from him by the desk barrier. The arrangement shown in the right part of the figure removes that barrier, presumably encouraging a more friendly relationship with the visitor.

Barriers interfere with relaxation.

White (1953), a cardiologist, carried out an interesting study in his office. On half the days he sat so that his desk was a barrier for the patient. On the other half he moved his position so that there was no barrier. He called patients who sat using the chair back "at ease," and those who sat on the chair edge as "ill at ease." White found that with the barrier only 11 percent sat at ease. Without a barrier 55 percent sat at ease. One might expect that such reactions would reflect important feelings about the visit.

Hitler was a jerk.

Charlie Chaplin in the movie *The Great Dictator* gave a beautiful example of how furniture and furniture arrangement could be used to control the social relationship. Mussolini, who was visiting Hitler, came into Hitler's office. As the office was extremely long, visitors had to walk in the open a great distance to the huge desk. At the desk sat a visitor's chair with legs so short that the visitor had to look up at Hitler. In the scene Mussolini sat on the back of the chair, looking down at Hitler.

Reread the chapter summary at the beginning of the chapter.

DISCUSSION

1. Is a client/prospective user an object of design, a source of information, a participant in design, or what? What should he be?

2. In a brief study in the concourse of our student union, an interior design student found the following group sizes:

Number in group	Number of groups	Percent of total people
1	125	22
2	93	33
3	50	27
4	16	12
5	6	5
6	1	1

If such group sizes are typical, by what techniques, in various types of spaces, might such group sizes be accommodated?

WHERE (OR HOW) DO PEOPLE SIT?

The subject here is the evaluation of seating arrangements. Based upon actual behavior, can you confirm any of the chapter "principles" or discover any others?

Impressionistic Observation

Visit a few different types of spaces to observe the occupants' behavior. Keep in mind the concepts from the chapter: territoriality, crowding, spatial invasion, marking, sociofugal, sociopetal, social distance, group size, barriers, facing the music, personalization. What subjective impressions do you have about what was going on in the spaces? Write a brief paragraph of your impressions of each space.

Plan of Study

Based upon your impressionistic observations select some particular aspect to study (such as facing behavior). Plan how to study this by making objective observations. Generally speaking good observations are not gathered willy-nilly. Your plan of study should include at least the following items: (1) A statement of the specific problem you are concerned with, for example, to determine the facing behavior of patrons in Cardinal's Cafeteria. (2) A statement telling how you are going to gather appropriate observations, including where you will be and when you will observe, and an appropriate form for tabulating observations.

Observations and Report

Make your observations. The report should include: (1) The raw data as tabulated on your forms. (2) Any data analysis, such as totals and percentages of different group sizes. (3) Whatever conclusions you draw from the study. (4) Any design recommendations based upon your results, such as "place only two-person tables in the cocktail lounge."

REFERENCES

FLYNN, J. E., T. J. SPENCER, O. MARTYNIUK, and C. HENDRICK. Interior study of procedures for investigating the effect of light on impression and behavior. *Journal of the Illuminating Engineering Society,* 3(1):87-94, 1973.

HALL, E. T. *The silent language.* Garden City, N.Y.: Doubleday, 1959.

KLEEMAN, W. Behavioral change on Ward 8. In *Proceedings of Symposium on Environmental Effects on Behavior,* Big Sky, July 1975.

KNAPP, M. L. *Nonverbal communication in human interaction.* New York: Holt, Rinehart & Winston, 1972.

LAWRENCE, J. E. S. Science and sentiment: Overview of research on crowding and human behavior. *Psychological Bulletin,* 81(10):712-720, 1974.

SOMMER, R. Small group ecology. *Psychological Bulletin,* 67(2):145-152, 1967.

SOMMER, R. *Personal space: The behavioral basis of design.* Englewood Cliffs, N. J.: Prentice-Hall, 1969.

WHITE, A. G. The patient sits down: A clinical note. *Psychosomatic Medicine,* 15:256-257, 1953.

5

Larger Spaces

"To design requires talent but to program requires genius."

LE CORBUSIER.

The design of larger spaces is based primarily on the desired spatial relationships among the activities that make it up, in order to maximize the performance of them. In preparation for design, the designer must get an understanding of the organization. Information must be gathered: activities must be identified, with their desired interrelations and design requirements. Layout proceeds from activity interrelations information to produce a schematic diagram. Space requirements can then be used to produce layouts. These are then the basis for design. Computer programs have been developed to help the designer by generating alternative layouts.

In designing individual workplaces, consideration of the human body is taken to achieve efficient performance and to minimize discomfort. In designing smaller spaces, social-motivational considerations generally dominate the arrangements. Here, with larger spaces made up of workplaces or smaller spaces, we are primarily concerned with their jux-

In designing larger spaces, floor planning is paramount.

taposition (floor planning) in order to maximize the performance of the total set of units or the "system."

DESIGN PREPARATION

Design preparation involves understanding and information-gathering.

Two things should be accomplished during the design preparation (programming). One of these is to get an understanding of the organization to be accommodated by the design. The second is to formally gather information needed in planning. In some cases, focus on information-gathering may blind the designer to the fact that she doesn't understand how the organization works.

Organizational executives provide design objectives.

Design preparation would normally begin with a discussion with the executives of the organization. Usually a design is a redesign—either of the same physical space or for the same organization in a new building. What is it hoped to accomplish in the new layout? What problems exist in the present layout that should be overcome? What constraints are there on the new design? What data preparation has the organization done? Does it have detailed department specifications, preliminary layouts, drawings of the present space, organization charts, and job descriptions? These constitute the beginning of understanding the job and gathering information for design. In addition to studying these materials, the designer will want to observe the organization's operations and talk with its personnel to gain understanding and gather information.

Layout involves "transactions" and "activities."

In factory layout two types of design predominate. One is *product layout,* the other *process layout.* In product layout, exemplified by the assembly line, the arrangement is to permit the efficient production of a single product or a similar group of products. In process layout similar functions (such as machining) performed on many products are grouped together.

Most factories are mixtures. In a broader field of layout, we will speak of *transactional layout* and *functional layout*. In transactional layout we are concerned with arranging activities so that the important transactions of the place can be efficiently gone through, one step to the next (analogously to product layout). In functional layout related functions constituting an activity will be placed together. The major design questions are the relations of the several activities. In some organizations, crucial transactions will involve the dealings of members of the public with the organization, with the crucial functions being the internal workings of the organization.

Information Gathering

Three types of information need to be gathered: identification of activities, relationships among them, and requirements for their performance.

Identification. The transactions and activities that will be the manipulated components of layout out need to be identified. This identification may already exist (for example, the activities may be the departments of a company), or it may have to be developed in conjunction with organizational personnel.

Transactions and activities must first be identified.

In the case of transactions, the designer would like to identify a few cases that account for most of the fairly standardized activities. In a library, for example, frequent activities include coming in to use the card file, going into the stacks to get a book, checking out a book, coming in to use reference materials.

Important transactions should be studied.

Although it is common to have activities correspond to some organizational unit, such a correspondence is not always appropriate. In cases such as the layout of the home offices of a large corporation, a hierarchy of activities and sub-activities would be needed: Major corporate divisions might be activities, departments within divisions sub-activities, and so on.

Activities usually correspond to organizational units.

Basically, a big job can be broken down into sub-jobs of manageable size. In many cases activities will be individual workplaces. If there is a hierarchy, at any given level shoot for ten to 20 activities. Most crucial is not to have too many activities at one level.

Relationships

Transactions are related to activities.

Transactions may occur entirely within a single activity (say, checking out a book within the Circulation Department) and thus should be optimized as part of the detailed design of that activity. If a transaction involves several activities, the transaction should influence the *closeness-desired relationships*.

"Closeness-desired relationships" are crucial in layout.

Of primary importance in the layout are the closeness-desired relationships among activities. In factories the major consideration in deciding how close two activities should be together is material-handling volume (or some variant of this quantitative measure). That is, if activity J and activity P involve large and frequent movements of materials in either direction, money will be saved if J and P can be located close together. Konz, a Kansas State industrial engineer, has pointed out (in a personal communication) that this basis is probably overemphasized, because once some material has been "handled" the major cost has been incurred regardless of movement distance. However, it is important. In some cases, human traffic plays a similar role. In a high school frequent movements of large numbers of people occur and should be a basis for layout. Data can be gathered by traffic counts of people just as a highway engineer might gather data: How much traffic is there at a particular place; how many trips are there between the outside and the cafeteria? In most cases, however, the major basis for determining the closeness-desired relationships to be used in the layout is, and should be, subjective.

In the example shown in the box, "Specifications for a University Department," eleven activities and their requirements are listed, with a table that shows a closeness-desired judgment for all pairs of activity. Some person or people (preferably) are asked to decide for every combination of two activities which of four categories of closeness are wanted: "E" = "especially important," "I" = "important," "O" = "ordinary importance," or "X" = "undesirable." Thus, the "instrument room" that holds equipment for the classrooms and laboratories should be near them (closeness is "especially important"). As class groups may sometimes move from the classroom into the laboratory it is "important" to have these rooms close to each other. As there is no particular relationship between classrooms and the departmental offices, no special judgment is made. As a coffee room is partly a place to get away from work, it is judged undesirable to have it close to offices.

Judgments are usually the basis for closeness relations.

SPECIFICATIONS FOR A UNIVERSITY DEPARTMENT

Suppose the following activities and requirements have been defined for a university department:

A. *Classrooms.* Three rooms, for 20, 40, and 60 students. Use university rule of 15 sq. ft./student (thus, *1800 sq. ft.*). Lights should be dimmable. Chalkboards should hang on three walls, or provision for multiple boards in the front should be made. Boards should be separately lighted. A projection screen should be provided. Sound control should be superior.

B. *Laboratories.* Five larger laboratories (300 sq. ft. each) and five smaller laboratories (150 sq. ft. each) for student and faculty research (thus, *2250 sq. ft.*). All rooms should have dimmable lighting and superior sound control. The larger rooms should have electrical strips (110, 208 volts) on all walls, a compressed air outlet, a sink, a chalkboard, and a tackboard. The smaller rooms should each have electrical strips and a 0.25 sq. ft. porthole, one foot above the floor to the hallway, that should be closeable from both sides. The laboratories should be located on the ground floor.

C. *Instrument Room.* A space of *120 sq. ft.* to store audiovisual aids for the classrooms and instruments for the laboratories.

D. *Library.* A space of *360 sq. ft.* with 200 linear feet of book space, a chalkboard, and superior sound control. This room may be used as a classroom or seminar on occasion.

E. *Faculty Offices.* Ten offices, each 10 x 12 feet (thus, *1200 sq. ft.*), each with a window which opens and provides a view of earth and sky from a seated position in the center of the room. There should be a chalkboard and tackboard in each office and a tackboard outside each. There should be a coat hanger and 60 linear feet of book space.

F. *Department Offices. (1200 sq. ft.)* Provision should be made for eight workplaces, for the department chairman's office, an administrative assistant, the departmental secretary, a receptionist-typist, a typist, and a clerk and for a copier (noisy) and a reproducing typewriter (noisy). Department files and stationery must be provided for. The department chairman's office should have superior sound control. The receptionist-typist's position should be at the offices' entrance. The departmental secretary's position should be at the chairman's office entrance.

G. *Graduate Student Offices.* Spaces should be provided for 40 graduate-student desks at 30 sq. ft. per student (thus, *1200 sq. ft.*).

H. *Student Organizations.* Space for office use for student organizations *(60 sq. ft.).*

I. *Undergraduate Carrels.* Space for 16 undergraduate study carrels at 12 sq. ft. each (thus, *192 sq. ft.*). Preferably, carrels will not all be adjacent.

J. *Seminar. (330 sq. ft.)* A room to accommodate a conference table for 12 people, a clothes closet, a blackboard, a projection screen, dimmable lights, and superior sound control. May be used as a classroom.

K. *Faculty/Staff Coffee Room. (180 sq. ft.)* Provision for a table and chairs, easy chairs, cupboards, a sink and refrigerator, a window (as in faculty offices), and a tackboard and a blackboard. All spaces shall have individual thermostats. Total space = 8892 sq. ft.

Closeness-Desired Relations*

ACTIVITY	B	C	D	E	F	G	H	I	J	K
A Classrooms	I	E						I		
B Labs	—	E		E		I				
C Instruments		—								
D Library			—	I		I		I		
E Faculty Offices				—	I	I				X

ACTIVITY	B	C	D	E	F	G	H	I	J	K
F Dept. Offices					—		I		I	X
G Grad Offices						—				X
H Student Organization							—	I		
I Undergraduate Carrels								—		X
J Seminar									—	
K Coffee Room										—

Desired Closeness: E = especially important
                         I = important
                         O = ordinary importance*
                         X = undesirable

*"O"'s are not tabulated

Muther (1962), a Kansas City industrial engineer, who has been very influential in plant layout work and upon whose work much of this present scheme is based, uses more judgment categories. Here, we will suggest that if it is "absolutely essential" that something be placed next to a particular activity, then it should be part of that activity. Since the purpose of these judgments is to determine a differential basis for layout, roughly equal numbers of each category should be used (like the example).

Varying numbers of closeness categories can be used.

Requirements

Various other information that will affect the layout and the detailed design must be gathered or generated. The principal layout factor is floor space for each activity, which may be determined in several ways. An executive might say, "Make Department X the same size as S." The existing space allocations may be used, "Give Activity C about 10 percent more floor space than it has at present." Finally, detailed design could and usually should be the basis. In the example,

Activity floor space is an important part of requirements information.

the departmental offices should be laid out, workplace by workplace, to determine how they should be arranged and how much space that requires. This detailed design may be (and in this case, should be) a floor-planning exercise in itself. One precaution to take is to avoid being preoccupied with the present design—this new design should be better, and different as necessary.

Many types of requirements may exist.

Other requirements information that is needed is illustrated in the example. Any requirements for special lighting, sound insulation or treatment, ventilation, electricity overhead clearance, floor support, vibration isolation, access, and the like must be determined. In factories these data are crucial and frequently quite complex. More and more, with the growth of technology, such "special" requirements in offices, stores, and houses have also become important. As Williamson (1976), a Texas Tech architect and psychologist, points out, the numbers and types of people, furnishings, equipment, and any special environmental considerations (such as window orientations and views) are part of the required information.

LAYING OUT

Schematic Diagrams— Generating Alternative Solutions

A schematic diagram shows interrelations only.

The first layout step is to prepare a diagram, which may be called a *"schematic,"* "link," or "balloon" *diagram*. This diagram portrays the closeness relations among the various activities without showing the actual space requirements.

Start by picking the one activity of all the activities that has the most E's and I's. In the example, it is *B*. It has a E relationship with *C* and *E*. Now put down any other activities with E's; here, add *A*. Now add all activities that have I relationships with the activities already listed, that is, *A, B, C,* or *E* in our example. This adds *D, F, G,* and *I.* Add the remaining activities.

Procedures for diagramming are described.

In preparing the diagram, it will help to start by looking over the matrix for any clusters. In this case, *A, B,* and *C* constitute a "teaching cluster." *B, C, E,* and *G* constitute a "research cluster." Then, in actually making the diagram, try to place activities to one side or the other of a given activity in accordance with the clustering. The upper part of Figure 5.1 shows the

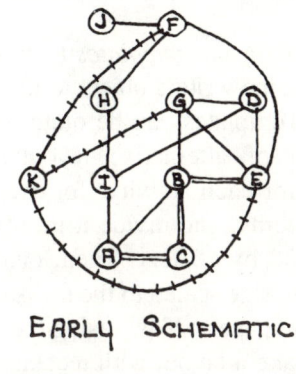

EARLY SCHEMATIC

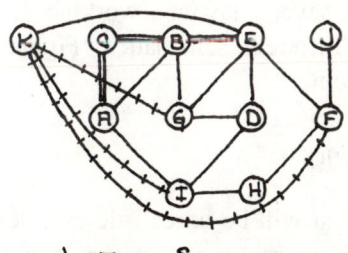

LATER SCHEMATIC

Figure 5.1 *Early and later schematics of a university department.*

first balloon diagram I made for this example (not counting a number of scratched-out false starts).

Now revise the diagram to simplify it. Basically, you want to avoid crossed and long "lines." For ex-

Schematics will need to be revised.

ample, in my early diagram, the *D-I* relation crosses two others, suggesting the need to get these two activities closer together. Then, the *E-F* diagram line is extended around several others. *E* and *F* need to be brought closer together. After a couple of intermediate steps of juggling, I ended up with the diagram given in the lower part of Figure 5.1. Except for the undesired relations to activity *K*, all crossed and extended lines have been eliminated. (If many undesired relations exist, it may be better to leave these off the diagram.)

Laying Out

Templates facilitate laying out.

For manual *layout, templates* ("cut-outs") are useful, although some writers object to them (as "unsophisticated"). Templates can be quite useful in aiding the generation of alternative layouts. Take the space specified for each activity, for example, 1800 sq. ft. for classrooms, and divide it into two dimensions, in this case 30 by 60 feet. Then, cut out a rectangle of appropriate size scaled to the measure of each activity. (I used grid paper.) Now, using the balloon diagram as a guide make a layout with rectangles. You may want to make several layouts, working from either one or several different schematics. Figure 5.2 shows my first layout.

Designing

The design will be based on the layout.

The layout will be unrealistic as a design for a building. For example, unless the layout is done on an existing building plan of doorways, hallways, restrooms, and the like, these will have to be added. Further, as Figure 5.2 illustrates, the layout results in an overall outline that one probably would not want to build. Further problems result from the arbitrary division of space requirements into shapes. For example, the specification of an outside window in each faculty

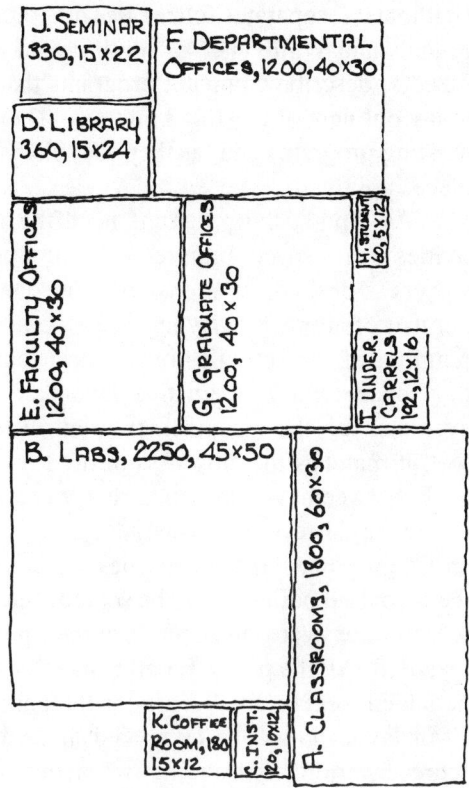

Figure 5.2 Layout of a university department.

office cannot be met using the present layout. More precise layout within each activity prior to the layout of the entire set of activities could avoid such problems. In any case, although a systematic layout approach can aid the designer, it in no way eliminates the designer. As the *design* is what will be built, it must try to account for all considerations.

COMPUTER LAYOUT

Once the information-gathering process has been completed, a computer can be used to do laying out

Computer programs exist for laying out.

(without a separate schematic diagramming step). Francis and White (1974), southeastern industrial engineers, describe computer programs that can be used to lay out new or existing buildings. There are several existing programs and, as they say, changes are taking place rapidly.

Layouts are generated and evaluated.

As inputs, the programs need the identified activities, the space requirements of each, and the closeness-desired relationships. In one program a number of alternative layouts are generated by random juggling of the activities over a grid representing the total space. Each alternative layout so generated is evaluated by the computer program in terms of how well it matches the closeness-desired relations. Thus, an E between two activities that were adjacent in a layout might receive two points, an I, one point, and an O, no points. If the activities were not adjacent in the layout no points would be scored. Similarly, if two X activities were adjacent, a minus point might be awarded. All the points for all pairs of activities would be added to get a total score for the particular layout. Each layout could be compared against a minimum score criterion, and alternative layouts can be compared against each other. As with manual layout, the designer then can select a layout and proceed to design.

Computer and human layouts are similar.

Figure 5.3 shows a sample computer-produced layout for a small factory. The upper part of Figure 5.3 shows the original layout. Based upon closeness-desired relationships derived from the flow of products through the factory, the computer program produced a number of layouts, including the one shown in the lower part of Figure 5.3 (most of them are rather similar). In addition to the activities shown, some "slack" space is shown, represented by "zeros." The computer needs extra space to have flexibility in planning, just as a human does. The result is similar to the human-produced layout of the university department,

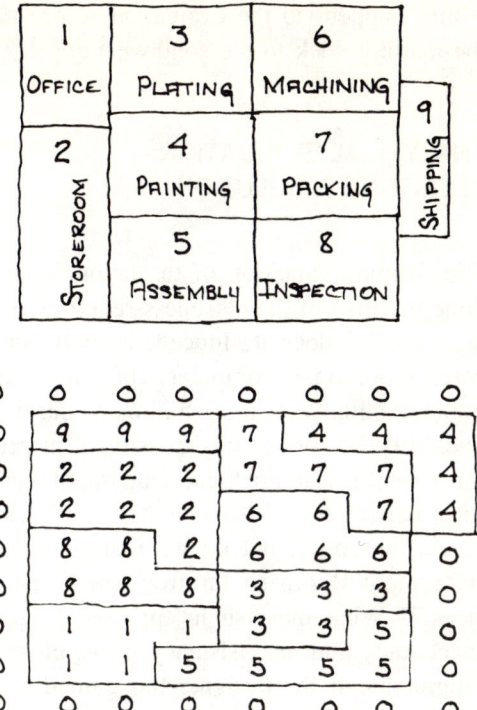

Figure 5.3 *An existing and a computer-produced layout of a manufacturing plant.*

except that the program alters the shape of the activities. (Sometimes the shapes are rather weird.)

What has been accomplished by the computer? The fairly rote procedure of deriving a layout from the closeness relations by a human has been done by the computer, with a similar quality. The advantage of the computer is that it can rapidly produce a number of alternative layouts from which the designer can select. Generation of alternative layouts "by hand" is not only time-limited but "imagination-limited."

The computer can give the designer many layout alternatives.

In one computerized layout scheme, called "interactive CORELAP," the designer can sit at the computer terminal and question the program, "What

The designer can interact with the computer.

would happen (to the evaluation score) if we moved the loading dock to the southwest corner?"

ANALYTICAL EVALUATION—SELECTING A SOLUTION

Layouts should be evaluated in terms of closeness relations.

The formal evaluation of the layout is probably best done in terms of the closeness-relations as the computer "score" does it. Indeed, as with any procedure carried out on a computer, the same result can be gotten manually. Although in many cases this "reproducibility" may be only possible "in principle," in this case it is also practical. One might want to have an informal review of the layout, too: "Yes, the layout meets the specs, but do we really want to have the Instrument Room so far from the Departmental Offices?" What most such "problems" will reflect is inaccuracy and inconsistency in the closeness-desired judgments. If the designer has gained a good understanding of the organization, she can avoid many layout problems by bringing unspecified constraints to bear on the design.

The layout is the basis for the design.

The layout becomes the basis for the design. The design, of course, can and should be examined in terms of all the design criteria. Several of these may have been incorporated in the earlier steps. (Two activities, one of them noisy, one an office, might be kept apart for health, performance, and discomfort reasons). Ultimately, however, one will want to explicitly evaluate the final design against all criteria.

DISCUSSION

In addition to the application described, what other design applications of computers have you heard of or can you imagine might be developed? What computer-using skills, if any, should designers have?

LAYING OUT

Select some layout problem (usually of some organization like the design department), and go through the steps up to alternative layouts and layout evaluation. You may want to work in groups.

REFERENCES

FRANCIS, R. L., and J. A. WHITE. *Facility layout and location: An analytical approach.* Englewood Cliffs: Prentice-Hall, 1974.

MUTHER, R., and J. D. WHEELER. Simplified systematic layout planning. *Factory,* 68-77, 101-118, 1962.

WILLIAMSON, H. H. Architectural programming. *Environmental Design News.* 7(3), 1-2, 1976.

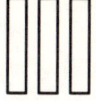

Environmental Effects

People are designed to survive within a quite limited range of the possible environmental conditions, for example, a range of temperatures. Within the survival range, a more restricted range enables satisfactory performance of activities. Within that range an even more restricted range is comfortable.

Except (possibly) for comfort, these limiting conditions are time-dependent. Although a person might survive an extremely low temperature for a short period, he wouldn't for a longer period.

A number of environmental conditions are not treated or not emphasized here because they are of limited importance in interiors. Acceleration, weightlessness and vibration are examples. Atmospheric contaminants, although important in factories, constitute a rather specialized topic.

The Luminous Environment

"The people I know still wear dark glasses indoors even though they fall over things."

E. BOMBECK.

Lighting potentially affects all design criteria. In extreme cases too much light might affect health and safety, but not generally. Luminance–which people see depends on illumination placed on a surface and surface reflectance. Seeing performance depends on detail size, contrast, the task time and accuracy requirements, age and other individual differences in seeing ability, and luminance. The designer controls luminance. Glare may produce disability and discomfort. Aesthetically pleasing lighting requires a number of light sources. Pleasing colors tend to be "cool," highly saturated, and lighter or darker than their backgrounds. Many suspected color effects are problematical.

Some animals are nocturnal and will work to get the lights turned off. Man, however, is primarily a daylight-seeing animal. Although he may prefer to do some activities in darkness, he is much more efficient at high levels of illumination. Whereas research, specifications, and controversy have focused on the performance criterion, all design goals are affected by

Light is critical for man.

illumination. The luminous environment, in contrast with the sound and thermal environments, can be a powerful tool in the hands of the designer to create spaces with positive impact on the users.

HEALTH AND SAFETY

Minimal light is needed for safety.

At this time there is not an abundance of research showing the health and safety implications of lighting, probably because of the absence from our usual environments of great extremes of light or darkness that might produce ill effects. Interest in lighting for safety has recently been stimulated by the Occupational Safety and Health Act. The Illuminating Engineering Society has proposed a set of minimum illumination levels (and a design approach, Kaufman, 1973) that depends on the amount of activity in an area and the potential severity of accidents. These levels, one-half to five foot-candles (0.46 to 4.6 dekalux), are so low, however, that normally in interiors—except in Los Angeles restaurants—they would impose little change. Of course, more illumination would increase the probability of seeing hazards and reduce the likelihood of accidents. In three European industrial studies reported by Sucov (1973), where in-force lighting was increased from about 15 to 100 footcandles, accidents dropped about 50 percent. If lighting is adequate for performance it will be adequate for safety. As lighting is optimized for performance it will also enhance safety, which is, behaviorally, an aspect of performance.

One question concerns too much light.

Lighting and health is a complex question. As virtually any substance ingested in sufficient quantity can be poisonous (or cause cancer), presumably extreme luminous environments might also. Indeed, with application to lasers and, less likely, high-intensity-discharge lamps, research is going on to determine dosages (duration by intensity) of light which will burn monkey retinas, and presumably human retinas. This is a far cry, however, from the claims by the opthalmologist Cogan (1968), (rebutted by Crouch, 1968) that the illumination levels for visual performance recommended in the U.S. were unnecessary for performance and harmful to eyesight. Cited in defense of this viewpoint was animal research such as that which showed that nocturnal animals like rats could be blinded by continued exposure to high illumination (a week of 1000 foot-candles or 930 dekalux).

At the other extreme, while countless parents have told their children, "Turn on the light, or you'll ruin your eyes," there is little evidence of such danger. A symposium held by the National Institute for Occupational Safety and Health had a number of experts discuss low levels of illumination (Heins, 1975). Research at Ohio State suggested that erratic eye movements may develop under low levels of illumination, which could lead to eye strain. One might apply the principle that that which is temporarily uncomfortable can produce damage over the long run, but more research is needed. Insufficient light may have nonvisual effects as well. Wurtman (1975) describes a number of health problems that may be treated with more light or be caused by insufficient light. The latter possibility exists because most living in developed countries takes place indoors where people have very little (artificial) light energy compared to daylight outdoors.

A question concerns too little light.

PERFORMANCE

Illumination and Luminance

So far we have been talking about *illumination* (or "illuminance"). If we have a light source (like a bulb)

Illumination usually decreases with distance.

and place a light meter at some distance from it, we measure illumination in foot-candles (fc) or dekalux. (One footcandle equals 1.076 dekalux.) Unless the light source is large in area, the farther away we get from it, the fewer footcandles we will measure with our meter.

Illumination on a surface produces luminance.

When illumination falls on an opaque surface and is reflected or when it falls on a transparent or a translucent surface and is transmitted through it, people see the brightness (or in physical terms the *luminance*) of the surface. A key relationship relates illumination to luminance:

Luminance equals illumination times reflectance (or times transmittance). If illumination is measured in footcandles, luminance will be measured in footlamberts. Reflectance (or transmittance) is a nondimensional coefficient. (It has no units.)

Reflectance varies from black to white.

In principle, reflectance varies between zero and one. A zero reflectance surface would reflect no light (would be perfectly black). (Correspondingly, a transmittance of zero is opaque—no light passes through.) A reflectance of one would reflect all light (would be perfectly white). (Correspondingly, a material with a transmittance of one is transparent—all light passes through.) In reality a matte-black construction paper reflects about 5 percent, and new white plaster reflects 95 percent. Newspaper and concrete reflect about 50 percent; skin reflects from about 10 percent to 40 percent from dark black people to light white people.

Although it is luminance that we see, practical seeing situations are specified in terms of illumination rather than luminance. (This can be done by assuming typical reflectances.) One good reason is that one can measure illumination with a light meter costing perhaps tens of dollars. Measuring luminance is somewhat more cumbersome and requires a photometer, which may cost thousands of dollars. The lighting requirements most universally known are illumination or footcandle requirements. For example, for reading "medium difficulty handwriting," 100-footcandles are specified.

A very important practical consequence of the luminance-illumination relationship for the designer is that if lighter surfaces (ceilings, walls, floors, furniture) are used they will reflect more light, and the room will be brighter. If dark woods, fabrics, and paints are used in places where important seeing is required, either more light will have to be provided, or there will be a risk of poor seeing.

Use lighter surfaces where seeing is important!

Light and Seeing

For decades it has been known that the ability to see detail depends on a combination of the following factors: As a size of detail increases, seeing improves. As contrast in lightness or darkness between the detail to be seen and its background increases, seeing improves. As more time to look becomes available, seeing improves. As the inaccuracy tolerable in the seeing task increases, seeing is easier. As age of the observers increases, seeing declines. As observers with better vision are selected, seeing increases. As luminance increases, seeing gets better. To some extent, these factors compensate for one another. For example, if we have older observers we might improve their performance with larger detail.

Seeing performance depends on several factors.

Frequently there is little control over most of these seeing factors: The detail to be seen exists, it's hard to enlarge, and we simply must see it. Contrast is whatever it is, and with some pencil writing, reproduction processes, and inspection tasks, contrast is very low. We want to do the task quickly and thus see as rapidly as possible. Similarly, some high level of accuracy is required. Usually, we have little control over the age or visual capability of the observers; we want most people to be able to see well. One factor we frequently can control is the light. We can apply more

The amount of light can be controlled.

light. When this not-so-young writer wants to read the small-print numbers in the campus telephone book, he holds them directly under a desk lamp, receiving 500 to 1000 footcandles.

Performance Research and Lighting Standards

Illumination standards are based on research.

Early illumination research was done on visual acuity (like reading the eye chart at the optometrist's office) or reading, by Tinker (1951) in the United States and by Weston (1943) in Britain. Work by Blackwell (1959), an Ohio State psychologist, and his colleagues is the basis for U.S. illumination standards. Blackwell's subjects judged during which of several time intervals a disc of light was flashed on a screen. Size, contrast, and duration were varied; and accuracy of performance was measured. A "visual task evaluator" was then taken into the field—into banks, dairy barns, operating rooms—and used to determine how difficult—compared to the laboratory tasks—the practical seeing tasks were. Thus, the amount of illumination required could be determined.

Provide light to enable the critical task.

These are task lighting standards. Thus, whereas in bank lobbies, in general, 50 footcandles (54 dekalux) are specified, in the teller's areas where much more difficult seeing tasks are performed 150 footcandles (160 dekalux) are needed. The "critical-task concept" says to light an area for the most critical (important and difficult) seeing task performed, not for the easier seeing tasks. Thus, people have sometimes been confused by the fact that (and research shows) they can read good print under very low illumination. Such reading is usually not the critical task in an area.

An international set of standards exists.

Recommended lighting levels have gone up over the years as we have learned more about lighting and seeing and as better light sources (such as fluorescent lights) became available. Illumination levels are generally higher in North America than in less affluent places like France. Work by a committee of the CIE (International Committee on Lighting) has resulted in international (unofficial) illumination standards reflecting the research and economic conditions of a number of developed countries, including the U.S., and may ultimately be adopted throughout the world. These recommendations are shown in Table 6.1.

Recently, because of the general lack of understanding of the basis for the footcandle levels, research on the relation between illumination level and performance of "practical" tasks like needle threading has been undertaken. Among others, Smith (1976), an Ohio State psychologist, and Chitlangia (1976) and Pangrekar (1976), Kansas State industrial engineering students, have conducted such studies. Figure 6.1 shows the general nature of the results of such studies.

Designing Lighting for Visual Performance

In an era when there is much talk about energy saving, yet good seeing requires good lighting, how shall the designer act? Lighting uses only a few percent of the energy consumed in the U.S. Even so, it shouldn't be wasted. By eliminating waste light, yet providing light to see, the designer can do a good job with design practices like using more efficient light sources such as fluorescent or high-pressure sodium lights rather than incandescent lights. Light not actually on tasks can be reduced, for example, by using more supplemental lighting, such as desk lamps, and less general lighting, such as built-in ceiling lights.

Practical tasks require more light.

More precise control over general lighting by more switching capability is also helpful.

Light should not be wasted.

A second area of concern facing the designer concerns lighting for aesthetics versus lighting for seeing. The designer may feel that a particular space, like an expensive restaurant, should have little illumination and variable (bright and dim) areas. The question she

Table 6.1.

(Unofficial) International Illumination Standards

Range	Recommended illumination		Type of Activity
	footcandles	(dekalux)	
A			
General lighting for areas used infrequently or having simple visual demands	2	(2)	—Public areas with dark surroundings
	3	(3)	
	5	(5)	—Simple orientation for short temporary visits only
	8	(8)	
	11	(10)	—Rooms not used continuously for working purposes, e.g., storage areas, entrance halls
	16	(15)	
	21	(20)	—Tasks with limited visual requirements, e.g., rough machining, lecture theaters
B			
General lighting for working interiors	32	(30)	
	54	(50)	
	81	(75)	—Tasks with normal visual requirements, medium machining, offices
	106	(100)	
	160	(150)	
	210	(200)	—Tasks with special visual requirements, e.g., hand engraving, clothing factory inspection
C			
Additional lighting for visually exacting tasks	320	(300)	
	540	(500)	—Very prolonged and exacting visual tasks, e.g., minute electronic and watch assembly
	810	(750)	
	1080	(1000)	—Exceptionally exacting visual tasks, e.g., microelectronic assembly
	1600	(1500)	
	2100	(2000)	—Very special visual tasks, e.g., surgical operations

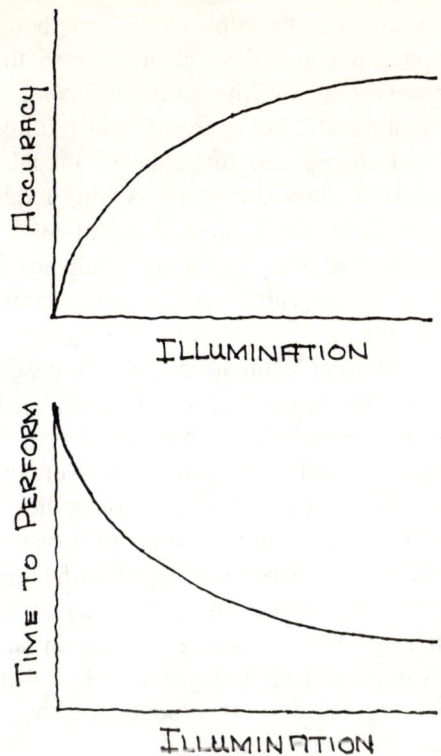

Figure 6.1 *Accuracy and time-to-perform with illumination.*

needs to ask is, "What is the critical visual task?" Although the work of the customers and waitresses in reading the menu and the bill may require the most light, it may be considered relatively unimportant. In this place, seeing one's companion's face in conversing may be most critical.

Determine the critical seeing task!

Calculating Lighting

When an illuminating engineer designs lighting for a space, he designs to provide a certain average level of illumination, say 100 footcandles (110 dekalux) in an office, maintained over a period of time. He uses a

Precise illumination calculations are possible.

method called, "the zonal cavity" method. He divides the space into a ceiling cavity (above the lights), a floor cavity (below the work surfaces), and a room cavity (the rest). The types of light fixtures, the room size and shape, and reflectances are taken into account. How dirty the space is (dirt reduces reflectances) and the maintenance program (such as cleaning lights and walls) are important. Light sources also degrade with age. Fairly precise calculations for design are possible.

One can quickly estimate fixtures or footcandles.

A simpler estimation procedure, described by General Electric (1971), may be used by the designer to estimate either (a) the number of fixtures of a certain type needed to provide some average number of footcandles, or (b) how many footcandles will be provided by so many light fixtures of a type.

Calculations are explained.

Table 6.2 shows the number of lumens of light produced by certain common light sources. A particular lighting fixture has one or more of such sources. For example, a fixture might have four 4-foot 40-watt fluorescent tubes, thus producing about four times 3,000 lumens, or 12,000 lumens.

The relationship is: Average illumination (fc) equals the total lumens per fixture divided by twice the area (sq. ft.), per fixture.

Suppose we had an office 40 feet by 50 feet, within which we wanted an average of 100 footcandles, using the 12,000-lumen fixture just described. How many fixtures would be required? Using our formula, 100 footcandles = 12,000 lumens divided by twice the area/fixture (in square feet), or:

$$100 = \frac{12,000}{2(\text{area/fixture})}.$$

Multiplying both sides of the equation by area/fixture, dividing both sides by 100, and dividing 12,000 by 2 and by 100, we get:

area/fixture = 60 square feet.

The number of fixtures required is found by dividing the room area (in sq. ft.) by the area/fixture (in sq. ft.). Here, we have:

$$\text{Number of fixtures} = \frac{(50)(40)}{60} = 33.3$$

We might actually use 34 fixtures in this office to get 100 footcandles, or some slightly different number of fixtures might be used to make the layout more convenient (say, 35 fixtures in a seven-by-five arrangement.)

Table 6.2.

Lumens produced by common light sources.

Type	Initial Lumens	Efficiency*
Incandescent		
25 watts, frosted	230	9.2
40 watts, frosted	460	11.5
75 watts, frosted	1,180	15.7
100 watts, frosted	1,740	17.4
200 watts, frosted	4,000	20.0
Fluorescent		
48-inch, 40 watts, cool white	2,950	75.6
96-inch, 75 watts, cool white	6,200	82.7
High Intensity Discharge		
Mercury, 40 watts	1,580	39.5
Mercury, 75 watts	3,150	42.0
Mercury, 400 watts	15,800	39.5
Metal halide, 400 watts	32,000	80.0
High-pressure sodium, 400 watts	47,000	117.5

* *Efficiency is given in lumens/per watt. Larger numbers indicate more light produced per unit of electricity. Therefore, the larger numbers indicate more efficient sources.*

The other type of calculation estimates footcandles produced by a given installation. Suppose a ten-by-twelve-foot office had two four-tube, 4-foot fluorescent fixtures. How many footcandles, on the average, would there be?

Illumination (fc) equals 4 tubes times 3000 lumens/fixture divided by 2 times the 120 sq. ft. office area, divided by two fixtures:

$$\text{Illumination} = \frac{4 \times 3000}{2(120 \div 2)} = 100 \text{ fc.}$$

In this case, because of the small size of the space and small number of fixtures, the estimation is less precise and the variability of illumination in the room is greater.

The designer can be sure there is enough light.

Using this technique coupled with the illumination recommendations in Table 6.1, the designer can determine that enough light is provided for the work in the space while selecting the type of fixture she feels most appropriate.

(DIS)COMFORT (GLARE)

Performance loss and discomfort can occur because of glare.

Two types of effect of overly bright and/or contrasting light sources are disability glare and discomfort glare. If a light source has sufficient illumination and is sufficiently close to the direction in which one is looking it may reduce one's ability to see (disability). It may also produce a discomfort effect. A familiar example is the presence of the high-beam headlights of an oncoming car on a two-lane road at night. (Where the duration of the glare source is brief, the effect is called "transient adaptation.") If one watched the same oncoming car in bright daylight, one might not even be aware of the headlights. Thus, the contrast of the light source with its background is important. Another factor is the size of the source—the larger it is, in general, the more uncomfortable it is. *The IES Lighting Handbook,* a broadly useful reference on all aspects of lighting, describes a rather involved method for evaluating lighting systems for discomfort glare. Some simpler rules of thumb for avoiding discomfort also exist.

Figure 6.2 shows one condition that should be met to avoid discomfort glare. If one has to look up as much as 45° (above the horizontal), then a tolerable light source may be as luminous as 2200 fL (7500 nits). People will rarely look up so high for very long. If the upward viewing angle is as little as 15°, then light sources only as bright as 500 fL (1700 nits) become comfortable. Here one is looking only slightly above horizontal and may more frequently look there, and for longer periods of time. This assumes the space is illuminated to at least 100 fc (110 dekalux).

Glaring luminance depends on position.

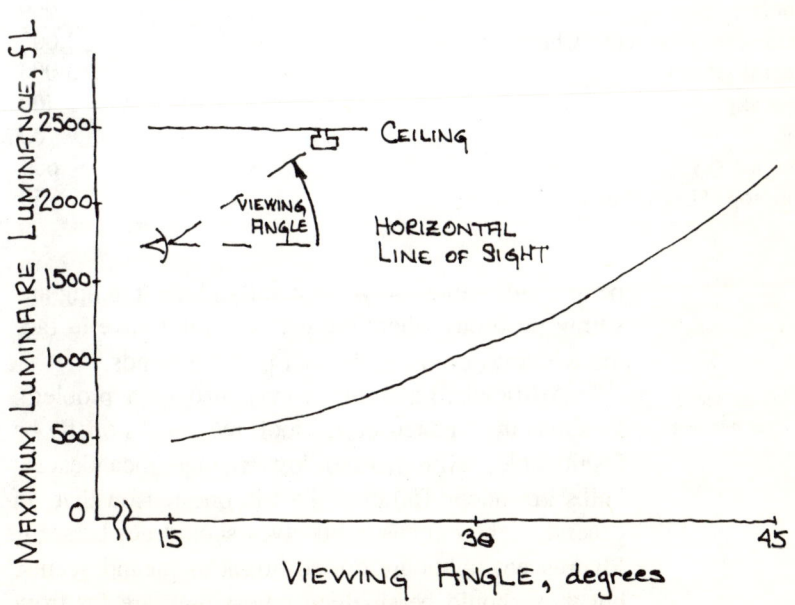

Figure 6.2 *Tolerable luminance with viewing angle.*

Windows may be glare problems.

How restrictive are these conditions? Table 6.3 shows the luminances of various sources. Although one would usually be willing to sit gazing out the window at the ground or buildings, if the ground were snow-covered or if the sun were visible the view might

Table 6.3.

Luminances of some light sources.

Source	Luminance, fL
lightning flash	30,000,000,000
Sirius (star)	4,000,000,000
nuclear fireball	1,000,000,000
sun (at meridian)	500,000,000
sun (near horizon)	1,800,000
incandescent bulb, frosted 100 watts	50,000
incandescent bulb, frosted 25 watts	15,000
snow field (at noon)	9,000
candle	3,000
fluorescent tube, cool white, 40 watts	3,000
general terrain	2-3,000
clear sky	2,400
moon	700
overcast sky	600
table top, 50% reflectance, 100 fc	50

be uncomfortable. So we generally place standing and sitting positions where the user does not have to face the windows or where he can pull the blinds.

Lights should not be seen.

Artificial light sources may also be a problem. Whereas the "naked bulb" look may occasionally be fashionable, even frosted low-wattage incandescent bulbs are uncomfortable. This is one reason that, in general, light sources themselves should not be seen. Fluorescent lights are not so bright as incandescents, but they should be shielded unless they are far from normal view, such as high overhead.

This discomfort may be aggravated in dimly lit, "romantic" places such as diningrooms, livingrooms and bedrooms, cocktail lounges, and expensive restaurants. First, the general illumination is usually low, not 100 footcandles. Second, incandescent lights are generally used. If these are not properly shielded, discomfort will result. In such darkened spaces even a candle may be annoying.

Glare is possible in darkened spaces.

An old set of rules of thumb for minimizing glare uses brightness ratios. For good seeing, we want high contrast between the task (say, printing) and its background (say, paper). Other than this we want low contrast. Between the task background (say, paper), for comfort, and the immediate surround (say, the desk top), we would like to keep the ratio of brightness less than three to one. As the task and its surround will generally have the same illumination, this means controlling the reflectances. Because the task will normally (and properly) have a high reflectance, the desk or table top should also be light. Further, the ratio of brightness between the task surround and the entire field of view should be less than three to one. Because the desk top should fairly light, the brightness ratio requires keeping most surfaces within a room where visual work is done also fairly light. These considerations (along with general considerations of efficiency of light utilization) lead to common recommendations that ceilings be virtually pure white, that walls and furniture have on the order of 50 percent reflectivity (be fairly light), and that floors and lower surfaces may be darker.

Minimize contrast in the space.

One case where brightness ratio rules are frequently violated is with recessed (usually fluorescent) ceiling fixtures. Such fixtures have been popular because they have been popular! They also give the ceiling a "clean," uncluttered appearance. As Fischer (1973) has pointed out, however, as the lights are recessed, no light falls directly on the surrounding

Recessed fixtures should be excised.

ceiling from them. In the daytime, in a room with windows, daylight will light the ceiling so that the light fixtures are not *relatively* too bright. At night, however, a glare problem will exist. On my campus, an interior room (no windows) was lit this way. The vice-presidents' secretaries who worked in the room complained that it was "too bright." Actually, it was "too contrasty."

AESTHETIC PLEASANTNESS

Flynn studied pleasantness of lighting.

A study of Flynn (1973), an architect at Pennsylvania State, and his colleagues in architecture and psychology at Kent State is of interest in revealing what is pleasant in lighting and how this relates to other aspects of lighting. They had a large number of observers judge a conference room at General Electric's Lighting Institute in Cleveland. The room had overhead diffuse (fluorescent) lighting that could be varied in intensity (from 10 to 100 fc), overhead downlighting (narrow-cone incandescent), and peripheral (wall) lighting. These systems could be used singly or in combination. The semantic differential as well as other judgment techniques were used. Three lighting factors or dimensions emerged.

Three factors were pleasantness, visibility and spaciousness.

An overall evaluation or pleasantness factor was found. More pleasant lighting consisted of combinations of different lighting systems. Best was the combination of overhead diffuse and downlighting and peripheral lighting. A visibility factor emerged—the more illumination the lighting system produced, the higher the judged visibility factor. The amount of illumination was *unrelated*, however, to lighting pleasantness. The third factor, spaciousness, was greater when peripheral lighting was used—when the walls were light. Spaciousness was also somewhat higher with illumination.

These findings are important in defining subjective reaction dimensions to lighting and are satisfying in relation to the "art" of lighting. Variations in light associated with multiple lighting systems square with other subjective reactions. For example, a moonlit, starry night and a sunny sky with some clouds are pleasant natural lighting conditions. Except in arid areas a uniform cloudy sky is unpleasant. (The designer of the rebuilt La Guardia airport terminal built a long, curved pedestrian concourse with the outer wall a continuous translucent glass of a uniform gray, like clouds and quite depressing.) The designers of places of leisure like cocktail lounges and restaurants frequently create a lighting environment of considerable luminous variability (sometimes too much so, causing discomfort glare).

Variety of lighting is important aesthetically.

In contrast, the lighting engineer has frequently created in the office and the store a highly uniform general lighting environment. (They say, "designing for *average* maintained illumination.") This is highly monotonous, but *flexible*. Desks or counters can be placed anywhere and receive sufficient light. With regard for energy sharing and aesthetics, this approach will change, in many instances to a lower level of general illumination with higher local levels and thus greater variation through supplemental lighting. New types of supplemental lighting fixtures undoubtedly need to be developed. Sucov and Taylor (1975) of Westinghouse's Research Laboratories report a study where subjects, surprisingly, performed a visual task better in a room with non-uniform light at the same level of light as in a uniformly lighted room.

"Engineered" lighting is frequently monotonous.

There has also been a tendency to use incandescent lights (low initial cost but high operating costs) exclusively in houses, in most cases providing insufficient light. In commercial establishments and institutions, it has been more typical to use fluorescents and other low-operating-cost sources (with high initial

The designer should be innovative in choice of light sources.

costs). The emphasis has been on visual performance with a tendency to ignore other criteria. Such wooden approaches need to be changed to consider other, different lighting techniques while trying to meet all design criteria.

COLOR

Many reactions to color are minor.

Color is clearly an important part of the luminous environment. However, probably more nonsense has been written about color effects than about any similar phenomena. Many writers confuse their strongly held beliefs with facts. In a large number of research studies carried out over the years, many seemingly contradictory results have been found. Some of this may be due to poor research, but the major reason is probably that many reactions to color are *very small effects*.

What Is Color?

"Color" is a misleading term because it is loosely used. Of several systems for describing colors, the Munsell system is most popular in the United States. There are three dimensions to color. *Hue* is the dimension that generally varies with wavelength of light, distinguishing such entities as "red," "yellow," "orange," "green," "blue," "purple," and corresponding to what is sometimes called "color." *Value*, the "reflectance," "lightness," or "brightness," describes a dimension of color that we have been discussing at length as a critical aspect of light. *Chroma* or *saturation* are terms for the third dimension of color, which varies with the purity or complexity of the combination of wavelengths of light that make up a given color. At one extreme a highly saturated hue, say a blue, would have a very narrow band of wavelengths—would be a very "rich" color (sometimes misleadingly called "bright"). At the other extreme, a completely unsaturated color has all wavelengths in it, that is, has no color, is white, gray, or black. A fairly unsaturated color is "faded" (like blue jeans). If it is also light it would be termed a "pastel."

Figure 6.3 shows a diagram portraying the way the three color dimensions are usually represented. Hue has been "wrapped around" the circle of the "color solid" or "color cone" so that the extremes of red and purple are bridged by the "extra-spectral" colors. If the hues are properly arranged, the hues on opposite sides of the circle are "complementary" or

The three dimensions of color are represented by a solid.

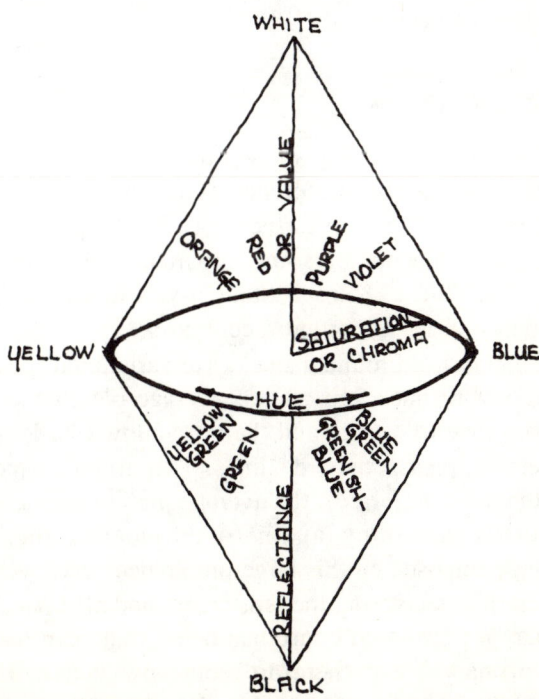

Figure 6.3 *Dimensions of color (color cone).*

"opposite" colors. Value, reflectivity, or lightness varies from top to bottom, from white to grays and hues of increasing darkness to black. Neither pure white or black can have hue (so the solid comes to points), but intermediate lightnesses can. The dimension represented from the centerline of the circle outward in any direction is increasing saturation. In the Munsell system, hues are represented by letters, such as "R" for "red" and "GY" for "greenish yellow." These letter designations may also be modified by numbers, such as "5R," to give finer distinctions. After the letters a number describes lightness. "Zero" is black, "10" is white. Finally, saturation is represented by a second number; "0" is unsaturated, and saturation is rated on up to a high of "14." (Some hues cannot be so highly saturated.). Thus a color might be designated "PB 5/7."

Color Preferences

Guilford and Helson did important work on color pleasantness.

The most commonly studied reaction to color is color pleasantness or preference. Guilford (1934, 1936, 1939, 1959) who was then a Nebraska psychologist, and his students did some important early work. Helson (1970), a Kansas State psychologist, has done some further important recent work.

"Warm" colors are less preferred than "cool" colors.

Guilford found a sine-wave variation of pleasantness with hue. Red was of average pleasantness. As we move to orange and then to yellow (the least preferred), pleasantness declines. Then to green and blue (the most preferred), the average preference increases, finally declining again to purple and then red. Superimposed on this large preference curve were lesser effects favoring the red, green, and blue hues. This may reflect some conscious belief that such hues are "primary" and therefore somehow better. Helson (1970) who used 125 "object" colors 35 years later, found a similar preference for green, blue, and purple hues.

For hues, Guilford found increasing preference for increasing lightness. He found that black, particularly, and, to a lesser extent, white were liked, with decreases in pleasantness toward intermediate gray. In Helson's study a methodological improvement was made: Observers judged the object colors against 25 background colors. This enabled discovery of Helson's most important finding: High lightness-contrast combinations of object and background colors were highly liked, low lightness-contrast combinations were little liked. That is, preferred combinations had light object colors with dark background colors, or vice-versa.

High lightness contrast leads to pleasantness.

Both Guilford and Helson found that the more highly saturated the object color the more highly preferred it was.

Saturated colors are preferred.

Helson also studied the type of illumination, for various types of incandescent and fluorescent lights. Only small effects on color likings were found. Generally, if a color was liked under one illuminant, it was liked under another. Of course, extreme exceptions can be shown. Jerome (1973) has also found that no one fluorescent color (warm white, cool white, etc.) is widely preferred: Substantial fractions of the population like each of the common ones. Judd (1971), who was with the National Bureau of Standards, gives illustrations of good and bad color combinations.

Color of light is relatively unimportant.

Two further characteristics of color preferences need noting. First, Helson showed likings for hues are continuous. That is, if a particular hue is well liked then adjacent hues will be fairly well liked also. Second, there is the question of how hues should be combined for pleasantness. One so-called law of harmony says that compatible hues are drastically different, not similar. Not so. Good combinations may be any de-

The matter of pleasing colors is a complex one.

The desirability of "bold" colors depends on their usage.

gree of similarity or difference. The designer must look at the colors and decide whether they look good together.

Finally, we should try to get some perspective on this color preference work. Do we always want to use highly saturated, cool colors with high lightness contrast? I think not. If the only basis for pleasantness is color, then highly saturated, contrasting colors give something to prefer. On the other hand, where other design elements are present as a basis for an aesthetic experience, as in a painting, we may not choose such drastic color stimulation, that is, a beautiful piece of art may have very subtle coloring. In modern nonrepresentational art, where spatial forms tend to simplicity, colors tend to be "bold."

Other Color Effects

It is believed that lightness and darkness affect apparent size and distance.

Various hypotheses are used by the designer with respect to color and apparent distance and size. For instance, a "too-high" ceiling might be painted a dark color to make it appear closer. Light-colored walls are supposed to make the room seem more spacious (walls recede).

Research on size, distance relationships is confusing.

An early study by Gundlach and Macoubrey (1931) showed a substantial relationship between reflectance of squares and their apparent size. Lighter surfaces were closely related to larger apparent size. Johns and Summer (1948), psychologists at Howard University, found that lighter colors are farther away when they seem the same distance as gray (thus, hue and saturation were confounded). Hanes (1960) reported substantial differences (15 to 20 percent) among small color samples when judged in the laboratory among "warm colors" ("advance") and "cool colors" ("recede") and between light and dark colors. Then Hanes, a Johns Hopkins psychologist, built a full-scale room with a whole wall that could be recolored and then moved in or out by the observer. (Hue, lightness, and saturation were confounded. That is, the few combinations used represented simultaneous variations in all three color dimensions.) Small or no effects were found in this room. McCain and Karr (1971), two U.S. Army researchers, found no luminance effects. They did find red is perceived as nearer than blue. Clearly, more research is needed.

Other possible color effects include "warmth" and "coolness" effects (Chapter 9) and various "emotionality" effects. For example, some years ago, a dean of women advised coeds not to wear red clothes for fear of arousing their dates. Today, I would say, "Don't depend on it!" A study by Wexner (1954) had judges relate "moods" to hues:

Colors are supposed to convey emotions.

> Blue: secure, comfortable, tender, soothing, calm, serene
> Red: exciting, protective, defending, defiant
> Orange: distressed, upset
> Black: despondent, powerful
> Purple: dignified
> Yellow: cheerful.

There is no doubt that somewhat consistent judgments of mood will be made, at least in one culture. The question is what further effects such colors may have. Wilson (1966) has reported somewhat higher galvanic skin responses (a sweating indicator of emotionality) for red compared to green slides.

Some studies have been done, and some uncritical reviews have been written. The effects are probably similar to alleged personality determinants in perception (projection) of color. Much is believed. The effects if any must be small, for little if anything has been proven. If a designed mood is desired and certain colors seem to fit, use them! Don't expect miracles.

Further research is needed.

DISCUSSION

Analyze a living room in terms of the activities that might be performed there as well as in terms of the various design criteria to determine (a) what sort of goals one should have for its lighting and (b) by means of what kind of lighting these design goals might be achieved.

LIGHTING THE DINING ROOM

Using the rough calculational approach, estimate the number of light fixtures needed for a "luxury-type" (expensive) commercial dining room. The room measures 50 by 50 feet. Each fixture contains one 25-watt incandescent bulb. It is desired to light the room as an "intimate-type restaurant with a subdued environment."

REFERENCES

ALLEN, E. C., and J. P. GUILFORD. Factors determining the affective values of color combinations. *American Journal of Psychology,* 48:643-648, 1936.

BLACKWELL, H. R. Development and use of a quantitative method for specification of interior illumination levels on the basis of performance data. *Illuminating Engineering,* 54:317-353, 1959.

CHITLANGIA, A. Effect of illumination level on work performance. Unpublished master's thesis, Kansas State University, 1976.

COGAN, D. G. Lighting, eyestrain, and health hazards. *The Sight-Saving Review,* 38(72):1-33, 1968.

CROUCH, C. L. Comments on Cogan's "Lighting, eyestrain, and health hazards." *The Sight-Saving Review,* 38(72):4-11, 1968.

FISCHER, D. A luminance concept for working interiors. *Journal of the Illuminating Engineering Society,* 2(2), 92-98, 1973.

FLYNN, J. E., T. J. SPENCER, O. MARTYNIUK, and C. HENDRICK. Interim study of procedures for investigating the effect of light on impression and behavior. *Journal of the Illuminating Engineering Society,* 3(1):87-94, 1973.

GENERAL ELECTRIC. *Industrial lighting.* Cleveland: General Electric, 1971.

GUILFORD, J. P. The affective value of color as a function of hue, tint and chroma. *Journal of Experimental Psychology,* 17:342-370, 1934.

GUILFORD, J. P. A study in psychodynamics. *Psychometrika,* 4:1-23, 1939.

GUILFORD, J. P., and P. C. SMITH. A system of color preferences. *American Journal of Psychology,* 72:487-502, 1959.

GUNDLACH, E., and C. MACOUBREY. The effect of color on apparent size. *American Journal of Psychology,* 43:109-111, 1931.

HANES, R. M. The long and short of color distance. *Architectural Record,* 127(4):254-256, 1960.

HEINS, A. P. *The occupational safety and health effects associated with reduced levels of illumination.* Cincinnati: Health, Education and Welfare Conference, 1975.

HELSON, H., and T. LANSFORD. The role of spectral energy source and background color in the pleasantness of object colors. *Applied Optics,* 9:1513-1562, 1970.

JEROME, C. W. The flattery index. *Journal of the Illuminating Engineering Society,* 2(4):351-354, 1973.

JOHNS, E. H., and F. C. SUMMER. Relation of the brightness differences of colors to their apparent distances. *Journal of Psychology,* 26:25-30, 1948.

JUDD, D. B. Choosing pleasant color combinations. *Lighting Design and Application,* 1(2):31-41, 1971.

KAUFMAN, J. E. (ed.). *IES lighting handbook.* (5th ed.). New York: Illuminating Engineering Society, 1972.

KAUFMAN, J. E. Lighting for safety. *Lighting Design and Application,* 3(3):6-8, 1973.

MCCAIN, C. N., and A. C. KARR. *Color, differential luminance and subjective distance.* Aberdeen Proving Ground, Md.: Human Engineering Laboratories, 1971 (Tech Memo 4-71).

PAUGREKAR, A. Relationship between illumination levels and visual performance, and the effect of age on visual performance. Unpublished master's thesis. Kansas State University, 1976.

SMITH, S. W. Performance of complex tools under different levels of illumination. Part I—Needle probe task. *Journal of Illuminating Engineering Society,* 5(4),235-242, 1976.

Sucov, E. W. European research. *Lighting Design and Application,* 1973.

Sucov, E. W., and L. H. Taylor. *Behaviors affected by non-uniform light distributions.* Pittsburgh: Westinghouse Research, 1975 (Scientific Paper 75-1C5-V1S1B-P1).

Tinker, M. A. Desired illumination specifications. *Journal of Applied Psychology,* 35:377-382, 1951.

Weston, H. C. Proposals for a new lighting code. *Transactions of the Illuminating Engineering Society* (London), 8:17-32, 1943.

Wexner, L. B. The degree to which colors (hues) are associated with mood-tones. *Journal of Applied Psychology,* 38:432-435, 1954.

Wilson, G. D. Arousal properties of red versus green. *Perceptual and Motor Skills,* 23:947-949, 1966.

Wurtman, R. J. The effects of light on the human body. *Scientific American,* 233(1):68-77, 1975.

7

The Sound Environment

"Now, that's enough."

        HORACE

Noise is an ever-increasing problem. There is a need to control both wanted sounds and unwanted noise. Noises that many people are exposed to for long periods will produce hearing loss. They may have other health effects. Noise produces speech interference by masking speech. Nonspeech effects of noise on performance are problematic, depending on at least the type of noise, the type of task, and the type of person. Annoyance effects are substantial, and in general they do not disappear with time. Both exterior and interior noise sources need to be dealt with in design.

Noise levels in the U.S. are said to be doubling every ten years. In addition to the millions who have been deafened, virtually all of us are annoyed occasionally by noise.

Proper design for control of sound enables us to hear desired sounds and to avoid unwanted sounds (noise). For most spaces hearing wanted sounds will be accommodated by controlling noise and by treating

Noise levels are increasing.

Design enables hearing of wanted sounds.

surfaces with a mixture of sound-reflective and sound absorptive materials. Design of larger spaces for speaking, music, and broadcasting is specialized, involves the shape and size of the space as well as its surface treatment, and should involve early consultation with an acoustic design specialist.

Sound like light varies in frequency, amplitude and purity.

Sounds vary in frequency, for example, for human hearing from 20 Hertz to 20,000 Hertz, just as light varies in wavelength (the inverse of frequency). The pitch of sounds depends largely on frequency, as hue depends on wavelength. The loudness of sound is related to the amplitude of the soundwaves. The latter is measured in decibels (dB, or sometimes we will specify dBA). Just as light (or color) varies in purity or saturation, sound may vary in purity from "pure" tones of a single frequency, through musical notes of relative purity to complex sounds including noises. Just as white, gray, and black "colors" are impure mixtures of all wavelengths, white noise is in principle an equal mixture of all frequencies.

Noises may be "meaningful."

White noise sounds a little like jet aircraft (without the high whine), rushing air or radio static. It is frequently used in laboratory research to simulate actual sounds. Machine noise will contain some sound over the hearing frequency range but have peaks of sound at certain frequencies that give it its characteristic "sound." Impulse noise consists largely of sound at high peaks of a few frequencies, such as from gunfire. Speech, which is often noise, consists of varying frequencies within the middle of the hearing range. "Meaningful" noise might be any of these noise types, but especially speech.

HEALTH

Hearing Loss

Figure 7.1 shows the hearing threshold for an adult with normal hearing in dB as a function of frequency.

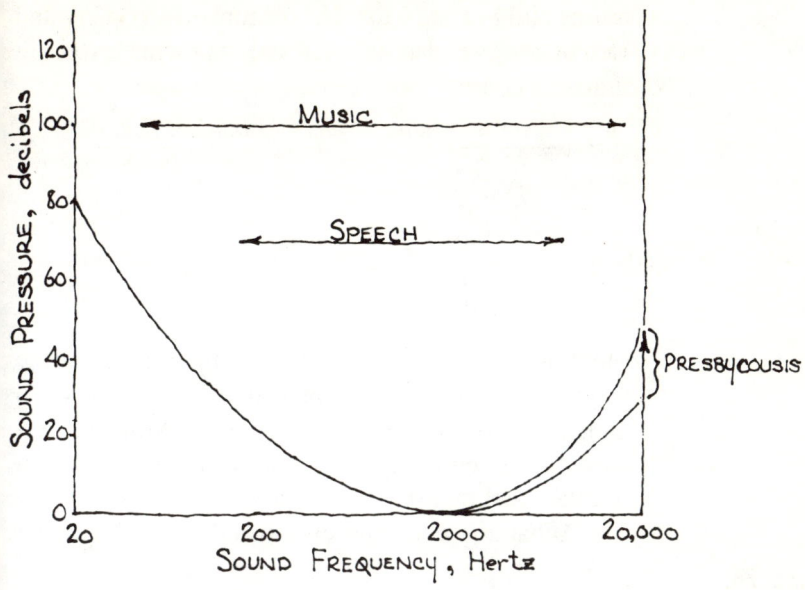

Figure 7.1 *Hearing sensitivity with sound frequency.*

What this curve shows is great sensitivity to sounds in the middle frequencies, with less sensitivity at high and low frequencies. The figure also shows the principal ranges of frequencies of speech and musical instruments, appropriately centered in the frequencies of sensitive hearing.

Hearing sensitivity varies with frequency of sound.

As people in our society get older, they experience a further reduction in sensitivity (raising of the hearing curve) at higher frequencies. The ensuing loss in hearing ability for higher-frequency music and for women's voices is believed to be due to exposure to a variety of noises of civilization. Study of natives along the upper Nile, where technology has been minimal and the environment thus quiet, shows little sign of such *presbycousis*. This difference might be genetic, or it may be due to the different levels of noise.

Continual exposure to noise reduces hearing with age.

In our society many people are exposed to loud sounds repeatedly over periods of years. Considerable evidence has accumulated concerning work-related

Work related noise can cause hearing loss.

noises and hearing loss. The Occupational Safety and Health program has adopted the following exposure limits to noise:

Sound level (dB)	Duration (hours)
90	8
95	4
100	2
105	1
110	0.5

Most people exposed to less noise than this over the years should not suffer appreciable loss of ability to understand speech. There are large individual differences in susceptibility to such hearing loss. Some authorities feel that these exposure levels are too high.

What do these exposures mean? Table 7.1 shows

Table 7.1.

Sound levels of various sources.

Source	Sound Level (dB)
Jet aircraft at 20 feet	140
Propeller aircraft at 20 feet	120
Chain saw at user	118
Riveting at operator	110
Power mower at user	107
Writer's son "quietly" practicing electric quitar	105
Loud motorcycle	105
Subway train at 20 feet	100
Food blender at user	95
Vacuum cleaner at user	85
Lathe at operator	81
Truck or bus at 20 feet	80
Food mixer at user	75
Conversation at 5 feet	60
Average office	50
Quiet office or residence	40
Broadcast studio	25
Threshold for 1000 Hz tone	0

some typical noise levels of various sources. Many factory noises, which may be above OSHA limits, tend to be ever-present during the work day. Many home noises are of brief duration and thus present little hearing loss risk. Many recreational sources are of serious magnitude. Thus, Lipscomb (1974) of the University of Tennessee, and speech specialists at Kansas State University report appreciable numbers of entering freshmen with significant hearing loss. At Kansas State, music, tractor driving, and shotgun shooting are thought to be primary causes.

Noises may occur at work, at home, or in recreation.

One of the problems with noise and hearing loss is that is is insidious. After exposure to a high dosage of noise a person *may* notice a *temporary threshold shift* (tts), that is, he may notice that he is temporarily less able to hear. But he will probably recover from this unless exposed again too soon. Over a period of time he may *not* recover; he may have acquired a permanent hearing loss. Thus, since there is no immediate and obvious consequent of noise exposure there is little motivation to protect oneself, either by reducing the exposure (turn the volume down, for example,) or, if that is difficult, by using ear protectors (which are uncomfortable).

Hearing loss creeps up on you.

Nonhearing Health Effects

Kryter (1970), a Stanford psychologist, has suggested that non-auditory health consequences of noise are minimal. He emphasizes various adaptive mechanisms that would protect the body. Indeed, this is a difficult matter to study because experiments on animals may not be generalizable to humans. Further, clinical studies of certain individuals who have happened to be exposed to noise and also have certain health problems are generally inconclusive in terms of cause and effect. Nevertheless, research has been done

Some evidence suggests nonhearing health effects of noise.

which suggests possible problems especially in the nervous and reproductive systems. The Welshes (1970) have edited a collection of papers on these effects. A conservative approach would suggest concern for the possibility of serious non-hearing health effects of sound.

PERFORMANCE

Speech Interference

Noise masks speech.

Anyone who has been in a noisy environment knows that it is harder to understand speech there. Considerable research has been done to give a detailed understanding of this phenomenon. Figure 7.2 shows a summary of some of this work. If the noise in a space were of some decibel level, say 60 dBA, then speakers

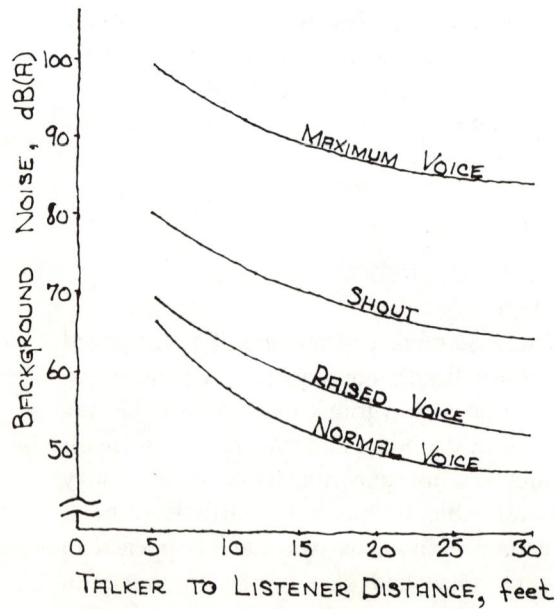

Figure 7.2 *Speech interference with listening distance.*

might be up to 8 feet apart while speaking in a normal voice, and still understand each other. At 100 dBA, some communication might still take place at less than 5 feet. Generally if the voice is about 5 dB above the background, communication will take place, The asymptote for "normal voice" suggests that, if the space were kept at about 40 dBA (as "quiet residence" or "quiet office" in Table 7.1) then an ideal speech environment would exist. An office at 55 dBA background would be just about at the limit of tolerance from this standpoint (again, Table 7.1, "conversation at five feet"—60 dBA).

General Performance Effects

Kryter (1950, 1970) and others have reviewed the research dealing with the effects of noise on non-auditory performance. It's a confusing picture. First, many different types of tasks that people perform have been studied. As noted, there are different types of noise. Further, what sound level constitutes "noise" and what constitutes "quiet" has varied. Finally, there are several loose "theories" about the psychological effects of noise, and indeed there may be several different types of effect. All in all, Kryter suggests that both laboratory research and studies of office and factory productivity have *failed* to conclusively demonstrate noise-performance effects, although annoyance or morale effects may be mechanisms for such performance losses or gains.

There are several "variables" in noise-performance effects.

Miller (1971), has summarized the summaries of noise effects on performance:

1. Steady (white) noises have no performance effects unless greater than 90 dBA.
2. Lower-intensity, irregular bursts may have performance effects.

Six factors in performance are listed.

3. Higher-frequency sounds have greater effects than those of lower frequencies.
4. Noise may increase the variability of performance. Thus, if work is machine-paced rather than self-paced, performance decrements might take place.
5. Noise may affect the quality rather than the quantity of performance.
6. Complex tasks are more likely to be adversely influenced than simpler tasks.

One might add that some effects may be transitory, taking place only at the beginning of the noise, and some effects may require hours to develop.

Distraction may produce performance loss.

There are at least two mechanisms that might be responsible for noise effects, distraction and arousal (or motivation). If one reads through the six numbered conditions just listed, each is consistent with the idea that although a performer may be attending to a task, noise of a certain type could distract him, thus producing poorer performance. Meaningful noise, especially speech, at low decibel levels, might very well distract one from a task requiring concentration. Thus, the student or worker in the open-plan school or office may be seriously affected by irrelevant but hearable conversations. Most research has not dealt with such noise.

Arousal may be a mechanism for performance effects.

Some noise-performance effects—good or bad—might be affected by increased arousal or motivation. Figure 7.3 shows a version of the "Yerkes-Dodson" effect. Task A is a complex, less well-learned task than task B. Starting at very low motivation or arousal, as arousal is increased one's performance of task A improves—to a limit. Thereafter, increasing motivation may be "too much" for this task, resulting in a decline in its performance. The same sort of thing happens with task B except that its performance continues to improve with higher arousal than A. Now, suppose that one effect of noise is to increase

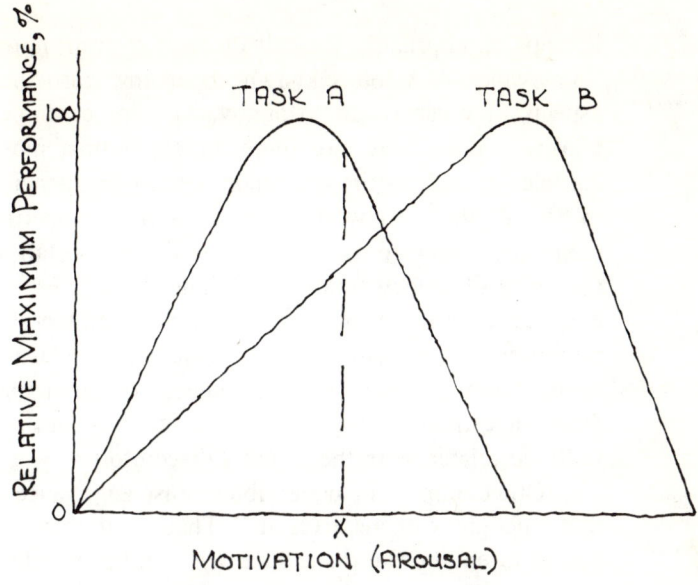

Figure 7.3 *Performance effects of motivation level.*

the general arousal or drive level or a person. If he were initially at level "X" and noise increased his arousal, his performance of task A would decline and his performance of task B would improve, thus, the possibility of "inconsistent" effects of noise on performance.

Kryter (1970), reports several studies that show an interaction between noise-performance effects and personality, specifically, with the degree of anxiety. Anxious subjects are more likely to show negative performance effects of noise. Anxiety itself may be interpreted as generally heightened motivational or arousal level. Add noise, and the anxious performer might be pushed so far out on the motivational axis as to be likely to show performance loss.

(DIS)COMFORT

Annoyance is related to speech interference.

Perhaps appropriately we call discomfort from noise "annoyance." A lot is known about how particular aspects of noise relate to annoyance. For example, relatively pure tones are more annoying than more complex sounds. More important, certain frequencies of sound, those to which the ear is most sensitive (hears the best), are most annoying. These also fall in the range of speech frequencies. Indeed, in assessing annoyance in offices an index was developed that explicitly was to measure the degree of speech interference. Although more precise indices for predicting annoyance are available, the dBA of sound is substantially correlated with the sound's discomfort.

Many people do not get used to noise.

One common misbelief about noise annoyance is that "people will get over it." That is, if they are forced to endure the disturbance, it will become less annoying. Beranek (1966) dispels this idea with data on residents subjected to aircraft noise. Over a period of time, one fourth of the people were *never* annoyed. One third of the residents did indeed get used to the noise so that the noise was less of a problem. One tenth of the people were *always* annoyed, that is did not get used to the noise. Finally, about one fourth of the people became *increasingly bothered* by the noise. So, although somewhat over half of those exposed to noise either never mind it or get used to it, over a third are always bothered or become more bothered. Unless we are willing to ignore the feelings of over a third of the people, noise annoyance should be taken care of.

Table 7.2 gives some dBA levels recommended by Fisher (1973) to avoid noise annoyance. One might note that these "tolerable limits" are frequently exceeded.

Noise limits are frequently exceeded.

Two areas of consideration exist for minimizing noise-producing speech interference and the corre-

Table 7.2.

Tolerable noise limits.

Type of Space	Sound Level (dBA)
Concert hall, theater	20
Classroom, sleeping room (!), large conference room	25
Living room	30
Private office	40
Restaurant, retail stores	45
Typing office	55
Workshop	65

sponding annoyance. Noise from outside the space must be controlled, and noise inside the space must be controlled. In certain cases these factors merge.

Aircraft noise has destroyed the usefulness of millions of homes, schools, and businesses (to the point of abandonment), but ground traffic from streets and highways is a more common problem. Although superior outside-wall insulation will help combat such noise, a generally better solution is not to locate too close to such sources. Until communities show greater responsibility in controlling noise pollution at the source and through zoning, site selectors must exert more discretion. In the case of multiple-occupant structures such as apartment houses, better sound-reducing partitions are the key to minimizing annoyance. Unfortunately the trend has been from better sound-reducing partitions to cheaper (and poorer) partitions even in otherwise expensive construction.

Within the space itself, again noise sources must be controlled. The use of carpets, draperies, and sound-absorptive ceilings will avoid the aggravation of noise in the space through sound reflections but

Outside noises must be controlled.

Inside noises must be controlled.

cannot be expected to eliminate significant noises in the space. Of course, in factories and to a great extent in offices and homes appreciable numbers of noise-producing machines exist. In many cases better floor planning could reduce the impact of these. Should a giant hammer be placed in the middle of a production area of relatively quiet operations? Should noisy computer printers and keypunches be placed in the office without regard to their noise impact? Noise sources should many times be isolated from all else by sound-reducing partitions.

Talk can be a hassle.

In offices, homes, and schools the final, and major, noise annoyance source is conversation where to some extent an open plan approach has been taken. No amount of surface treatment can solve this problem in most instances. In some open-plan offices where good outside noise source control has been obtained, annoyance from conversations within becomes intolerable because fundamentally the office is very quiet and thus all talk can be heard. In addition to hearing what one doesn't care to hear, there is the problem of perceived (and real) lack of privacy. "If I can hear him, he must be able to hear me." Sometimes background noise is introduced to mask such interfering talk, as either white noise or music, but this is like throwing sawdust on the floor to hide the dirt. The proper solution is to introduce sound-controlling partitions as needed. Nemecek and Grandjean (1973) report that over a third of the occupants of 15 Swiss open-plan landscaped offices were very disturbed by noise (mainly conversation) and only a fifth were not disturbed.

PLEASANTNESS

Background music may be pleasant sound.

By and large the major sound-pleasantness condition is music. Background music may have some behavioral effects as Konz (1968) has shown; it may mask noise; it may be pleasant. The major problem is that people have such diverse musical tastes that it may be difficult to please most of the people most of the time.

Other sounds are sometimes used aesthetically, primarily falling water. Frank Lloyd Wright designed a famous house overlooking a constructed waterfall. The water sound was so loud that the occupants rarely went outside.

Even geniuses make mistakes.

DISCUSSION

As noise is such a serious problem, causing health, performance, and annoyance effects, what can a citizen do to combat it? What can the designer of a home, office, school, or store do?

CAMPUS NOISE SURVEY

Visit a variety of campus spaces and off-campus hangouts. Using a sound-level meter set on the "A-scale," measure dBA at places where people are. (Illumination is measured at the task, not the eyes. Sound level is measured at the ears, not the source.) *Before* you measure sound level, use the following scale to judge the noise:

Noise-Annoyance

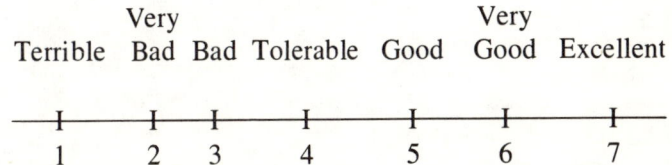

Making reference to Table 7.2 and your own judgments, which spaces have noise problems? From designer's point of view and from an "action" point of view, what should be done to correct any problems?

REFERENCES

BERANEK, L. L. Noise. *Scientific American,* 215(6):66-69, 1966.

FISHER, G. H. Current levels of noise in an urban environment, *Applied Ergonomics,* 4.4:211-218, 1973.

KONZ, S. A. The effect of background music on the control activity of an automobile driver, *Human Factors,* 10(3):233-244, 1968.

KRYTER, K. D. The effects of noise on man, *Journal of Speech and Hearing Disorders,* No. 287, 1950.

KRYTER, K. D. *The effects of noise on man.* New York: Academic Press, 1970.

LIPSCOMB, D. M. *Noise: the unwanted sounds.* Chicago: Nelson-Hall, 1974.

MILLER, J. D. *Effects of noise on people.* Washington: Environmental Protection Agency, 1971 (NTID 300.7).

NEMECEK, J., and E. GRANDJEAN. Noise in landscaped offices, *Applied Ergonomics,* 4.1:19-22, 1973.

WELSH, B. L., and A. S. WELSH (eds.). *Physiological effects of noise.* New York: Plenum, 1970.

The Thermal Environment

"He is well paid that is satisfied."

SHAKESPEARE

The fairly extreme hot and cold conditions necessary to endanger life or affect performance are mentioned. Various factors important to thermal comfort are described in some detail. These are dry bulb air temperature, relative humidity, air velocity, radiation, activity, and clothing. Whereas certain naturally occurring conditions are thermally pleasant, thermal comfort is probably a more desirable interior space design goal.

We produce energy in the body from the food we eat that enables us to perform activities ranging from sleep through lying still, sitting, standing, and various movements. In the face of cool environmental temperatures this energy also enables the body to maintain a relatively constant temperature (98.6°F or 37°C) as a core temperature (within the torso), with lesser temperatures in other places such as limbs and skin. The more active we are, the more heat we generate, keeping us warm in the face of low temperatures, and

Body temperature must be closely maintained.

127

people on severe diets get cold easily and like to take long, hot baths.

Heat transfer takes place through conduction, convection, and radiation.

We can gain or lose heat from the environment by several means of heat transfer. These include *conduction, convection,* and *radiation.* Conduction takes place through direct contact, especially with materials which are good electrical conductors such as metals. Generally, conduction is not very important in human heating and cooling. Convection, the most important means of heat transfer for people, takes place through the movement of liquids and gases, especially air movement. Radiation takes place at a distance without an intervening medium. There may be heat radiation from or to a window wall that is hotter or colder than room air temperature. Also, in certain workplaces there may be severe heat radiation to workers from furnaces or ovens. The usual mechanism by which we cool off in hot environments is by *evaporation.* We sweat. If the sweat vaporizes, we are cooled.

Key thermal factors are air temperature, humidity, air velocity, radiation, clothing, and activity.

Environmental conditions of significance to human thermal response are air (dry bulb) temperature (the normally reported temperature in degrees Fahrenheit, F, or Celsius, C), relative humidity (the percentage of moisture the air is holding compared to the maximum possible moisture content at that temperature), the air velocity (in feet per minute or miles per hour), and the presence of radiation sources. The other significant factors are insulation (clothing) and activity level.

Thermal comfort is key in interiors.

Thermal comfort is the most relevant criterion for interior spaces, but brief mention will be made of the other criteria.

SAFETY AND PERFORMANCE

Figure 8.1 shows our tolerance for extreme temperatures (under clothed conditions) as a function of time.

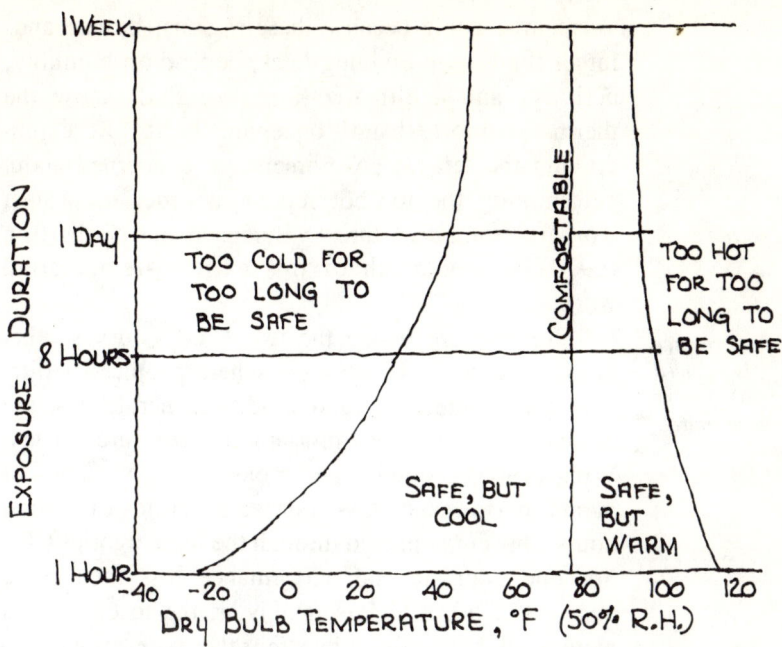

Figure 8.1 Tolerance and comfort with temperature and duration.

The right-hand curve shows that we can endure (stay alive) at temperatures as high as 90°F (32°C) indefinitely and temperatures above 110°F (43°C) for brief periods. The left-hand curve shows we can stand temperatures as low as 50°F (10°C) indefinitely and as low as −25°F (−39°C) for a brief period. Healthy, appropriately dressed people can tolerate these extreme temperatures, but McPherson (1973) reports that deaths in hospitals increased when room temperatures went outside the 60-80°F (16-27°C) range. The center vertical line suggests that comfort, regardless of duration, occurs at 78°F (25°C). The regions on the far right and left are too hot or too cold for the given duration to be safe. The inner regions are too warm or too cool for comfort. Actually, all three of these lines—"too hot," "too cold", and "comfortable"

Extreme heat and cold can be hazardous.

—are misleading because these regions, broad bands rather than sharp dividing lines, depend on humidity, activity, and acclimatization. We shall show the thermal comfort "band" or region shortly. Researchers and the federal government are concerned about determining the too-hot region in order to protect workers from heat threat. Berenson and Robertson (1973) survey much of this extreme-temperature work.

Performance is reduced at extreme temperatures.

Somewhere inside the two "too" curves other lines could be drawn to show where people's performance is affected by heat or cold. In general, these are at fairly extreme, uncomfortable temperatures. Thus, Wing (1965) plotted a curve based on 15 studies of mental performance loss. For work periods of several hours, this curve passed through the high eighties (°F). For one hour, mental performance loss took place above 95°F (35°C.) Presumably, if the research data were available, similar lines for other types of work in heat and in cold could be drawn. While a couple of recent studies have suggested some slight performance losses at more typical (but warm) room temperatures, quite extreme temperatures are usually required to reduce people's performance. There may, however, be an "air-conditioning distraction" effect. That is, in affluent societies, we have become accustomed to air conditioning (and, of course, heating) to achieve comfort. As conditions become somewhat too warm or cool we may be distracted by our discomfort from our task. Well-motivated workers would not experience such losses. Fox (1967) reviews some of the types of performance effects due to cold, while Jones (1970) reviews studies on heat effects. Jones concludes: "Existing data do not possess sufficient validity or reliability to allow prediction of the magnitude, direction or significance of performance decrement under thermal stress."

One kind of effect of note to the interior space

designer is reported by Griffitt and his student Veitch (1971), who found that under high temperature and crowded conditions, subjects were less happy and less likely to like another (hypothetical) person. Both effects—as Freedman (1975) suggests for crowding alone—may intensify any existing feelings, whether these are positive or negative.

Hot conditions may "sour" life.

THERMAL COMFORT

Considerable research has been done to establish environmental conditions that are thermally comfortable. In the most recent research, thousands of college students and older people of both sexes sat quietly reading or game playing for three hours, voting each hour on how cold, hot, or comfortable they were under some particular thermal conditions. Although there are wide individual differences in conditions at which people report comfort (with no single thermal comfort point), sex and age are unimportant factors. Figure 8.2 is based upon this work, as reported by Rohles (1971), a Kansas State psychologist.

The curves show that people report comfort over a range of temperatures in the upper seventies (°F), and are only "slightly cool" or "slightly warm" in dry bulb temperatures ranging from 68°F (20°C) to 86°F (30°C). We can be comfortable at a wide range of temperatures.

Thermal comfort is generally achieved in the high "seventies."

Two key findings relate to humidity. First, comfort was only slightly dependent on humidity, as there was a change of only 4 degrees F (2 degrees C) for the wide range of humidities studied. Second, a very wide range of humidities (15 percent to 85 percent) can be comfortable if the temperature is varied slightly, in contrast to some statements that the humidity should be around 50 percent. (Actually, in interiors, physical damage may result, furniture fall apart, and shoes mil-

Humidity effects are limited.

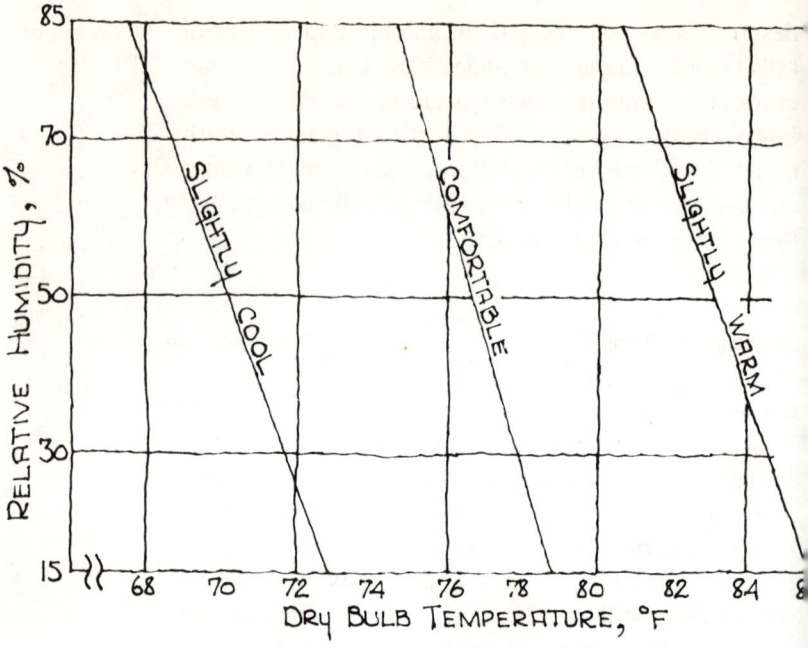

Figure 8.2 *Thermal comfort with temperature and humidity.*

A range of air velocities is desirable.

dew, if too-extreme humidity conditions are maintained. There may also be health effects from dryness.)

The American Society of Heating, Refrigeration and Air Conditioning Engineers (ASHRAE), which sponsored this research, suggests various adaptations to special conditions (Nevins and Gorton, 1974). These studies were done at 30 to 45 feet per minute (44 fpm equals one-half mile per hour). It would be undesirable to decrease air circulation much below this, as smells would linger. Air velocity can be increased another 100 fpm if the temperature is increased 5 degrees F. Very high velocities are uncomfortable at any temperature. This is for sedentary conditions. For heavy physical work, velocities up to 5 mph may be desirable.

If the room surfaces are cooler or warmer than the

air, radiation will result. For every degree of difference of average wall temperature, one degree of change of air temperature should be made to compensate. (Warmer air for cooler walls and vice-versa.)

Compensation for radiation may be needed.

Activity and clothing should also be taken into account to achieve thermal comfort. Temperature might be dropped as much as 12 degrees F (7 degrees C) if the occupants were very active. The comfort curves are based on "lightly dressed" people, say, in clothing equivalent to slacks and a shirt. As clothing is increased or decreased, comfortable temperatures decrease or increase. For example, if space users were dressed in heavy business suits or the equivalent, the temperature might be dropped 4 degrees F (2 degrees C). If occupants were nude, the temperature should be raised 6 degrees F (3 degrees C) to maintain comfort. This temperature, 84°F (assuming 50 percent humidity), corresponds well to the 82°F (28°C) bed temperature that McPherson found comfortable for sleepers. Obviously, increasing or decreasing clothing and thus reducing heating and air conditioning is a significant way to reduce energy consumption.

Clothing and activity level should be considered.

BEYOND COMFORT

Many who can afford it and others flee from northern winters to Florida and other sunny and warm climates. Although many factors are confounded in this subject, thermal pleasantness, as opposed to mere thermal comfort, is a major reason. Few go to Minneapolis in the winter for the weather. What is thermally pleasant? In addition to the common conditions that allow thermal comfort with a minimum of clothing, sun radiation is probably a major factor—both as a thermal condition and as a luminance condition. Northern skies tend to be cloudy all day with many a discouraging word. Although it would be possible to simulate

Certain conditions are not merely comfortable but also pleasant.

such conditions indoors with artificial lighting (as is done in some plant-growing research), health threats due to long exposure to sunlike lighting probably makes it undesirable. It would also expend a lot of energy.

DISCUSSION

1. An architect once described a visually beautiful building that sat unshaded in the hot Barcelona sun. "How," he said, "can one think of aesthetics at 120°?" Discuss.

2. Figure 8.3 shows a graph of results of various thermal comfort studies (recommended dry bulb temperature) as a function of the year of the research. How can you account for the changes?

THERMAL SURVEY

Go into a number and variety of spaces. Using a psychrometer, measure dry and wet bulb temperatures at various occupied working posi-

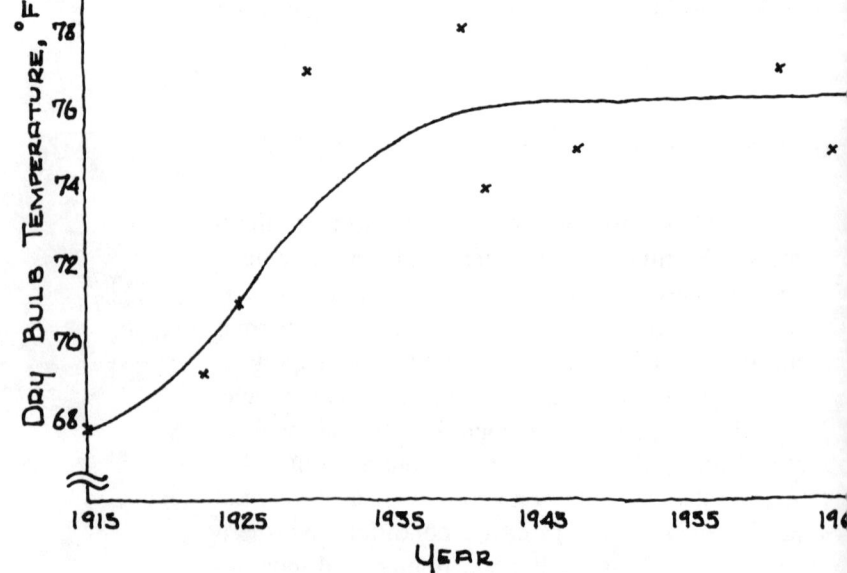

Figure 8.3 *Thermal comfort over the years.*

tions. Before revealing the temperatures, have the occupant vote on his thermal condition:

1. cold
2. cool
3. slightly cool
4. comfortable
5. slightly warm
6. warm
7. hot.

Note any relevant modifying factors: activity level, amount of clothing, apparent air velocity, any radiation sources. Convert your data to dry bulb temperature and relative humidity using Figure 8.4. In the figure find the vertical line corresponding to dry bulb temperature. Find the slanting straight line corresponding to wet bulb temperature.

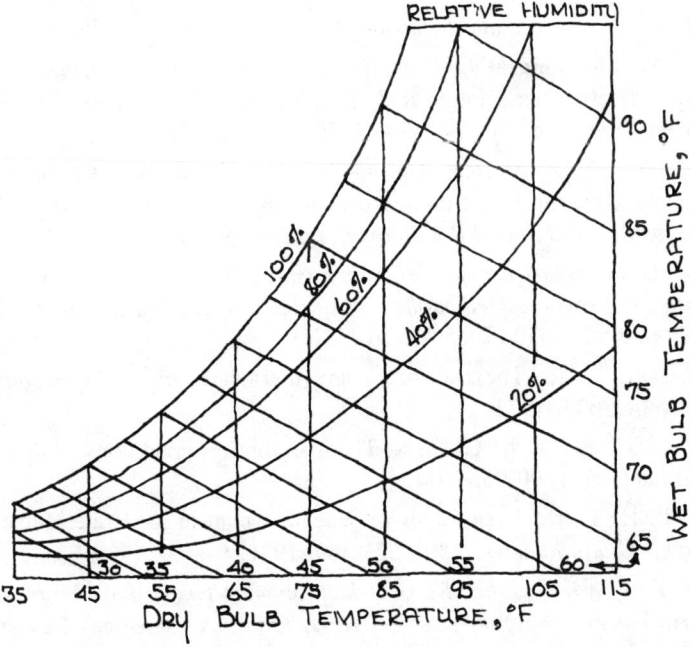

Figure 8.4 *Nomograph for dry bulb and wet bulb temperatures and relative humidity.*

Where these intersect, estimate the (curved line) relative humidity. Prepare a graph (like or on Figure 8.2) with dry bulb temperature on the horizontal axis and relative humidity on the vertical axis. Using everyone's data, plot and identify by number all the positions that were judged "4," "3," etc. Connect points with the same numbers ("isothermal sensation" curves). Do your results seem to agree with the Kansas State research results? If there are major discrepancies, how might they be accounted for?

REFERENCES

BERENSON, P. J., and W. G. ROBERTSON. Temperature. In J. F. PARKER, and V. R. WEST, (eds.). *Bioastronautics data book*. Washington: U.S. Government Printing Office, 1973.

FOX, W. F. Human performance in the cold. *Human Factors*, 9(3):203-220, 1967.

FREEDMAN, J. *Crowding and behavior*. New York: Viking, 1975.

GRIFFITT, W. Environmental effects of interpersonal affective behavior: Ambient effective temperature and attraction. *Journal of Personality and Social Psychology*, 15:240-244, 1970.

GRIFFITT, W., and R. VEITCH. Hot and crowded: Influences of population density and temperature on interpersonal affective behavior. *Journal of Personality and Social Psychology*, 17(1):92-98, 1971.

JONES, R. D. *Effects of thermal stress on human performance: A review and critique of existing methodology*. Aberdeen, Md.: Human Engineering Laboratories, 1970 (Tech Memo 11-70).

MACPHERSON, R. K. Thermal stress and thermal comfort. *Ergonomics*, 16(5):611-623, 1973.

NEVINS, R. G., and R. L. GORTON. Thermal comfort conditions. *ASHRAE Journal*, 16(1), 90-93, 1974.

ROHLES, F. H. Thermal sensations of sedentary man in moderate temperatures. *Human Factors*, 13(6):553-560, 1971.

WING, J. F. *A review of the effects of high ambient temperature on mental performance*. Wright-Patterson AFB, Ohio: Aeromedical Research Laboratory, 1965. AMRL-TR 65-102.

Putting It All Together

This final section includes three topics of importance to the designer. First, there are two important roles for research: Broadly applied research by scientists such as psychologists can obtain information useful to designers. Scientists and designers themselves can evaluate how well a built design worked as a basis for better design in the future. Second, designing is a creative and problem-solving process that is partly learned and can be improved. Finally, the design must be sold to the client. Otherwise, the designer might starve to death and no one wants that.

Research and Design

"All applied research is simulation."
                CORWIN BENNETT

Ergonomic research may confirm or deny common design "principles" or it may pin down their meaning. Evaluation research tests how well a particular space works or compares several spaces. Broadly applied ergonomic research varies in terms of whether the researcher tries to influence behavior or not, and whether and what kind of controls are used. Experimental evaluations, which may be conducted by the designer, need to avoid confounding of design features. An intuitive basis for statistical inference was suggested. Research subjects reacting to being in a study may be a problem, and nonreactive techniques are sometimes possible. Interview and questionnaire usage in evaluation is discussed.

THE ROLE OF RESEARCH

"Hues near the red end of the visible spectrum (reds, oranges, yellows) are 'warm' colors and those near the purple end (purples, blues, greens) are 'cool' colors."

Most people agree that reds are "warm," blues are "cool."

This hypothesis, which might be called "the hue-heat hypothesis," predicts people's reactions or behavior in response to an element of design. People will somehow feel warmer or cooler depending on the color of the space. If you asked a lot of people whether this is true, practically everyone would agree. Is it true? Maybe, depending on what is meant by "warm" and "cool."

No thermal comfort responses to color were found.

Paule Rey, a Swiss physician, and the writer designed an experiment to test the hue-heat hypothesis. If reds are warm, then people who see red surroundings, at a given temperature, should feel warmer than if the surroundings are normal or blue. Similarly, people looking at a blue environment should feel relatively cooler at the same temperature. Experimental subjects were put in an environmental chamber, sitting next to the walls, which were changed from 60°F to 100°F and back on a given "run." Each subject had three runs. On any run some subjects had red goggles on, some blue, some clear. At one minute intervals the subjects voted on a seven-point scale as to how hot or cool they were. What happened? Nothing. There were no differences among the thermal comfort judgments as a function of the color of the goggles.

No thermal color effects have been found.

Other research has been done on this problem. In one study subjects looked for long periods at a wall lighted with different colors. In that study body temperature was measured. Color made no difference. In another study, a subject performed a simulated driving task in one color of light. The subjects were told, "Oh, by the way, our heat control system isn't working, so please manually adjust the temperature so that it is comfortable." No differences in heat selection occurred as a function of color.

People do believe that colors are warm and cool.

Suppose you felt a certain room should be "warm" and decorated it in "warm" colors. A visitor comes into the room, and says "Oh, this is a nice warm room." Your selection worked. What you cannot do is turn the thermostat down because the room looks warm. Presumably we learn to believe the hue-heat hypothesis because we have been exposed since childhood to heat sources like fires, the sun, and stove burners that are reddish. To a lesser extent we have associated cool objects like vegetation and water with greens and blues. Then we have overgeneralized to consider most objects of such colors as warm or cool.

What has been the role of research for the designer? In this case research has pinned down, more specifically than we could otherwise do, just what the limits of color are. Research could test out other intuitive design bases. For example, it is believed that light surfaces appear farther away than dark surfaces. Thus, one might paint a "too-high" ceiling black in order to reduce its apparent height. Will it work? We don't know. If the belief is widely used as a basis for design, then its validity should be tested.

Ergonomic research can verify our intuitions.

Another, more positive, research role is illustrated by a study by Wools (1970). Wools had several ideas about what makes a room seem friendly. These features were the slope of the ceiling, the size of the windows, the arrangement of seating, and the style of the furniture. Sketches were made of rooms involving variations in these features. People then judged how friendly each room was. Sloped ceilings, larger windows, open seating (vs. having a barrier table), and more leisurely looking furniture all contributed to room friendliness. In this case, by his research, Wools has shown some techniques that contribute to the appearance of friendliness. The research didn't think up the friendly room features, Wools had to do that. The research showed which features worked; the designer generally has to guess.

The role of research is varied.

Canter (1970) has edited an excellent collection of ergonomic research illustrating many points discussed here.

Finally, quite different from this broadly applied

Evaluation tests whether specific spaces work.

research is evaluation. The designer has designed one or several store interiors. They are built. *Evaluation* looks at the specific spaces(s) and how it (they) worked. Did the combination of incandescent spots and recessed fluorescents blend well? Was the open arrangement of the office and store floor satisfactory, or was there too little privacy? Was the carpeted surface in store A worth the extra cost over the tile in store B? Psychologists are trained in research techniques and are thus best suited for the broad research. A designer, however, may very well do evaluation research, perhaps with some consulting assistance.

TYPES OF RESEARCH

Applied research has useful ends intended.

There are various ways of categorizing research. One of these is as basic or applied. *Basic* (or sometimes "fundamental" or "pure") *research* is done without any intention on the part of the researcher of solving some practical problem. *Applied research* is intended to have useful ends. Neither type of research is inherently more important or better than the other. As noted, applied research may be more or less broad in scope. Here we shall deal only with applied research.

There are three types of behavioral research.

It's convenient to divide behavioral research into three types—*naturalistic observation, correlational studies,* and *experimentation*–in terms of manipulation of behavior and type of controls.

Naturalistic Observation

Naturalistic observation involves unobtrusive observation of behavior.

Wide publicity has been given in recent years to cases of ethologists going up African mountainsides for a year or two to observe the behavior of gorillas or baboons or some other interesting species. This naturalistic observation is "natural" because it involves the subjects in their usual habitats, which are interesting and rich, rather than in zoo cages, which are sterile and dull. The observer attempts to be unobtrusive, not to influence the behavior of the subjects, although this is difficult with advanced species. (With human subjects such as the aborigines of Bomi-Bomi, the researcher may try to make a virtue of this difficulty by being a "participant observer.")

Sommer (1969) did some naturalistic observation in mental institutions and bars to find out how arrangements affected social behavior. Generally, the only "control" used with this method is careful observation, usually by a trained observer. Nothing very conclusive comes of naturalistic observation, but it is quite useful as a source of ideas or hypotheses that can then be tested by another type of research. The designer should make a practice of spending some time just watching to see what goes on in the kinds of spaces she usually deals with. What do people do when they first walk in a shop? When people are closely examining cloth, what do they do? If the designer is really going to design for people, she needs to be sensitive to the actions of people.

Naturalistic observation is a source of ideas.

Correlational Studies

Keck (1970) analyzed the records for 70,000 "at bats" in 22 major league baseball parks during one season. The daytime batting average was 0.258, while the average "under the lights" was 0.244. That is a substantial difference. Keck suggested that it was due to the inadequacy of the artificial ballpark lighting compared to daylight. One may immediately wonder, "Yes, but couldn't the difference be due to something else?" Perhaps the temperature has an effect, or people are physiologically more efficient during afternoons than in the evenings. Actually, Keck considered a number of alternatives to the lighting and did a rather

Correlational studies do not show cause and effect.

convincing job of discounting them. However, a fundamental limitation of the correlational method is that the fact that one condition is correlated with another (lighting with batting) does not mean that the one causes the other. There may always be alternative hypotheses.

A correlational study example.

Walters (1970) did a correlational study in Britain of railway train noise and residence location. Two things were measured at various distances from the tracks. Noise level when a train was passing was measured. It varied from 100 dBA at 15 meters (about 50 feet) to 80 dBA at 350 meters (about 1200 feet). A ten-item scale of annoyance was also administered to residents. A mean annoyance score of eight was found at 50 meters (150 feet); it went down to about a score of zero at 450 meters (1500 feet). Distance, sound level, and annoyance can now be correlated. In this case, presumably, a fairly well understood relation exists between distance and sound level (certain phenomena of physics) and between sound level and annoyance. The findings should provide a basis for planning how close to build houses to railroad tracks.

Correlational studies are useful for broad design questions.

As with naturalistic observation, in correlational studies there is the attempt to avoid influencing the behavior. Unlike the two examples discussed, correlational studies frequently involve sophisticated statistical methods. Considerable specialized statistical training is needed to use some of these. Correlational approaches are probably the most appropriate for broader research on design questions.

Experimentation

In an experiment the researcher tries to influence behavior.

In contrast with the previous types of research, in behavioral experimentation, the researcher sets up two or more conditions *(treatments)* and normally expects to influence behavior. For example, many years ago a college professor played records of readings of Greek poetry to his two infant sons during their mealtimes. When the sons had grown, he had them memorize various Greek poems, including the recorded ones and some others. The sons were able to learn the ones they had been exposed to as children easier than the others, despite the fact that the poems were meaningless to them both as children and as men.

Hill (1970) did an experiment on screen-mesh openness as a function of desired privacy with windows. An apparatus was used so that the subject looked out a window with either a landscape view or a view of a pedestrian walkway. He was told either to imagine that this window was in his bedroom or his kitchen. The subject then adjusted the screen mesh openness to a density he thought was appropriate. When the landscape view was given, subjects used somewhat more open screening than with the walkway view. A substantial difference was found between the choices of screen density for a bedroom and a kitchen window. This study of window screening provides the designer with actual screen light-transmission properties that might be used for privacy purposes in different situations.

An experiment may provide design details.

Evaluation

Although experimentation may involve sophisticated statistical and other skills, the logic is straightforward and may sometimes be employed in evaluation studies. Most evaluations, however, are *tests,* that is, just one condition is assessed for its satisfactoriness. For example, an open-plan school was designed and built: How well does it work?

Most evaluations are tests of a single space.

To turn an evaluation test into an experiment on open-plan schools, one would need at least one comparison test of a closed-plan school. Then the key would be that the two schools would be identical in all relevant respects except for the open or closed plan

In experimental evaluations of several spaces, confounding must be avoided.

characteristic. Many experiments evaluating open-plan offices have been nearly worthless because of confounding in a before-and-after experimental design: A company has an old, more-or-less closed-plan office. They build a new open-plan office. Various measures of goodness are gotten comparing the two offices. The open-plan office appears better. The trouble is, the old office was old, the new one is new. The new office was made larger to accommodate growth. Whereas the old office was just a building into which office furnishings were put, the new office was designed and decorated to be functional and pleasant. These other important differences are *confounded* with the openness feature so that the effects cannot be distinguished as to cause. The evaluation study is really a *pseudo-experiment* in this case.

Mock-up!　One particular kind of evaluation that should be done during the design process is the *mock-up*. Despite the design know-how that exists on many aspects of design—lighting, seating, and floor planning, for example—there is still the need in many important cases to build a mock-up to see how it works. Although this might be a scale model, sometimes a full-size mock-up, as of a typical office, will help to avoid later expensive dissapointment.

Evaluate!　The evaluation study, whether test or experiment, should be considered by the designer for her work in any instance where funds can be found to do it. Because of the small cost relative to the design and construction, sometimes the client can be talked into paying for an evaluation. Or perhaps some other way can be found to write off the costs. For example, some university professor might be talked into doing an evaluation on his own time.

STATISTICAL INFERENCE

In an evaluation study the researcher might say, "I'm interested in how this particular design worked, period." In most research there is a bigger question. For example, "We want to find out whether office workers are more productive in carpeted offices." Not in these offices only, but in general. This type of question calls for *inference*. The offices actually studied are a *sample* of offices in general. Offices in general constitute a *population*. We want to infer from the results with the sample to the population. To do this we need to have a *representative sample,* that is, one with the same characteristics as the population as a whole.

Usually in research we want to infer from a sample to a population.

One way to get a representative sample is to draw a *random sample*. This means each population member has an equal chance of being drawn in the sample. If all the members or their names are available a random sample can be drawn. For instance, all the clerks in a given department store would be such a population. A crude way to do this is to draw names out of a hat.

Sometimes one can sample randomly.

For some populations like all the housewives or househusbands in the U.S., there is no listing. There may be information on the population: how many are under 20, 20 to 30, and so on; how many are black, how many white, and so on. These data can be used to get a stratified sample, that is, a sample with certain percentages from each subgroup or stratum. This is what pollsters do.

For large, complex populations, sampling may be stratified.

Finally, things besides people can be sampled. In principle, one could get a representative sample of all the offices in Kansas. In practice, it would be very difficult.

Suppose we had samples of one hundred each of women and men in a study of thermal comfort. At various times they were exposed to various temperatures and voted on their degree of coolness–warmness. Suppose that the average temperature for "comfort" of women was 76° F and the average for men was 75° F. One might ask if this small difference

Statistical inference helps decide whether sample differences are "real."

for the sample would hold up if one could test the whole population. Suppose, for example, *all* women in the sample said they were comfortable at exactly 76°, and that *all* men in the sample said so at 75°. Most of us would say of this (fantastic) result that there must be a sex difference in comfortable temperature. Suppose, however, that the range of temperatures voted comfortable by both women and men was 60° to 100° F, with the respective means at 76° and 75°. Now we would be less certain that this is a "real" difference. Statistical inference is the use of certain statistical procedures to help the researcher make such decisions.

Statistical assistance can be gotten.

If sampling is used, the designer may need to use statistical inference, especially if her experimental evaluation is comparing several spaces. Statistical assistance is widely available these days. If the evaluation includes all of the users then no statistical inference is required, although statistical help in summarizing the results may be desirable.

REACTIVITY

In the Hawthorne illumination study, workers reacted to being studied.

It is clear that sometimes people in a study *react* to the fact that they are in a study rather than to the treatments *per se*. The classic example of this is the Hawthorne illumination study done in the 1920s at the Hawthorne plant of the Western Electric Company near Chicago. Increased lighting was introduced in part of the factory to see if productivity would increase. It did. It was increased further, and productivity increased further again. Finally some genius thought, "What would happen if illumination was decreased?" It was, several times. Productivity *increased* each time, until a very low level of illumination was reached. What happened? The women in this area could see that they had been singled out for special attention in an era when, generally speaking, management's only interest in workers was how much they could exploit the workers. The women appreciated the special attention and reacted to it by increasing their output. Parsons (1974) has recently questioned the authenticity of the "illumination study," but in any case, it makes a good story to illustrate reactivity.

In most studies where the subject knows he is in research, he tries to figure what the researcher is trying to do. In many cases the general idea of the study is patent. Usually the subject wishes to please the researcher by giving him the results he believes the researcher wants. A former student of mine had taken part in a thermal comfort study where subjects were asked to report their coolness or warmth every half hour. "It was obvious," she said, "that they wanted us to change our votes, so although my comfort hadn't changed, I changed my vote." Actually, it's unlikely that the researcher wanted the subjects to change their votes (unless, of course, they did feel differently), but a reactive effect has taken place in this case. In most evaluations, which would almost necessarily include interviews or questionnaires, there will be reactivity.

Nonreactive studies and measures are possible and should be developed in interior ergonomics. For example, Weixelman (1973), who was a student of this writer, wanted to determine the influence of sign size and position on the probability that the sign would be noticed. He placed signs of different sizes in different positions in a hallway of the student union. These signs said, "FREE BEER." Positioning himself outside a doorway where sign viewers would pass, Weixelman questioned two hundred people to determine if they had seen a sign and what it said.

One nonreactive indication of frequent importance to design is the unobtrusive, simple observation of people's movements within a space. Webb and colleagues (1966) have described a number of other non-

The subject may wish to please the researcher.

Nonreactive studies are possible.

Various nonreactive measures can be devised.

reactive techniques, some of which are design-relevant. In a museum for children, nose and finger prints on exhibit-case glass were noted to assess the popularity of particular exhibits. Degree of wearing of the floor tile would indicate the same thing. During the early days of TV, program popularity was noted by the peak loads of water usage as people used their bathrooms during commercials. (In Britain, peak electrical loads served the same purpose as people used their electric water heaters to make tea.) Garage personnel were asked to note at which stations car radios were set. City and other records exist on many behaviors. Some market researchers have scavenged garbage cans to determine liquor sales by brand according to empties. Bar sales are supposedly indicators of times of tension. (The taverns near our campus get busier and busier as exams approach.) Children asked to draw Santa Claus drew him larger and larger as Christmas approached. Various physiological indicators reveal the degree of interest or arousal of the person. For example, the pupils of the eyes increase in size with interest and emotion. The pupils of heterosexual males will increase, for example, when looking at pictures of nude women (and vice-versa). J. Payne (1970) has used this pupillary effect to assess reactions to interiors.

Interviews and Questionnaires

Opinions: ask the man who has one.

A psychologist, Gordon Allport, once said, "If you want to know what a man thinks, ask him." And, indeed, the reactive techniques of interviews and questionnaires are necessarily popular in space evaluation and other ergonomic research.

Interviews are expensive.

When do we interview, when do we use questionnaires? We interview if we are just exploring the topic (perhaps as a basis for preparing a questionnaire), if we have only a few respondents, or if we have a lot of money. Interviews take time and should be conducted by someone with a special background in the subject being examined. Usually a questionnaire is prepared for the interviewer to follow. The prepared interviewer will be familiar with the questionnaire and trained not to react (thus causing further interviewee reactions).

Public opinion pollsters use interviewers to select a sample according to certain procedures and to overcome the reading and writing limitations of large segments of the general populace. (According to Kilty (1976), one assessment showed that over 50 percent of U.S. adults were either incompetent readers or read with difficulty.) If loss of many respondents is no problem, if many people are to be questioned, if the relevant population is highly literate—like a college or white-collar group—then questionnaires may be more appropriate.

Use questionnaires with many people!

However people are to be questioned, a common tendency is to just start asking or writing down questions on the subject. The result may be a lot of irrelevant information as well as crucial missing data. As with most enterprises, one should start by setting down his information objectives for the interview or questionnaire. Then questions should be written to meet those objectives. A student once brought her friend in with a questionnaire about bedrooms, which he said he was interested in designing. Most of the questions asked for details about the respondent's sexual practices. Although sexual behavior along with sleeping and dressing is an important bedroom activity and should be a basis for design, not all details affect design. Unless one merely wants to find out what people are doing, a more explicit reference to questionnaire objectives would be desirable.

Start with your objectives.

In actually writing questions, there has been a lot of research, and there is a lot of art in doing it right. Books such as one by S. L. Payne, *The Art of Asking*

Avoid biasing questions.

Questions (1951), should prove useful. Two major ends shape the question. The most important is to avoid biasing the responses. Second is to get either statistical data or individualistic ideas and feelings.

If one asked, "Do you think the addition to the library is poorly designed?", probably many people would say, "Yes." If asked whether the addition was well designed, many would again agree. If one really wants to know how people feel he might better ask, "What do you think of the design of the new addition to the library:

excellent
good
fair
poor
very poor."

Questions may be structured or unstructured.

"Seventy-five percent of the people say the design of the new addition is excellent or good." Such a statistic gives a definite overall idea of opinions about the design. Now, why do people like it? Two possibilities exist: We can ask another *structured question:* "I like (or dislike) the new library addition because of:

spaciousness
noisiness
etc."

If by some means—your own observations or previous interviews—you feel you know the major good and bad points you may list them in such a *structured question.* An alternative is to ask an *unstructured* or free-response *question:* "Why do you like or dislike the new library addition?" The advantage of the unstructured question, of course, is that you may learn something new: "The building is too crowded into adjoining Denison Hall." "The entrance should have been placed higher, both to look better and to improve internal circulation." If you hadn't thought of these possibilities before, then the free-response question was informative. I like to follow a structured question with a free-response question. Some researchers object to unstructured questions because the researchers don't know how to fit the results into their computer program.

Interviews and questionnaires should be pretested. First, their length should be determined. Unless the subject matter happens to be fascinating, like your sex life, the time required should be small —perhaps 10 minutes for a questionnaire, a little longer for an interview. Clarity should be determined. Do the sentences make sense? Are there words that many people don't understand? Avoid slang, uncommon words, and technical terms like "spaced out," "esoteric," and "exhedra."

Pretest to determine duration and communication.

SUMMARY

Pay your do's!

Do support ergonomic research! Do carry out evaluations of spaces! Set down for each of the design/evaluation criteria specific goals. List any special aspect of the space that should receive attention. Make observations and measurements and ask questions. Consult with experts for help. (See the space evaluation exercise that follows.)

DISCUSSION

1. How wide should a hallway be? How could research be designed to answer this question?

2. Here are some hypotheses I published in *Environmental Design News*. These are statements made in various books on interior design. Discuss whether they would be worthy of testing by research and how this might be done:

Low tables and bedroom sofa—heighten the room's sense of vast, horizontal space.

Warm color of wood—creates a pleasant, inviting atmosphere.

Light marble slabs of the floor—add to the room's elegance.

A patterned ceiling—appears to advance and seems lower.

A painting on the ceiling—gives the illusion of a lowered ceiling and a more intimate room.

Plain light walls—give a feeling of spaciousness but may lack interest.

Horizontal lines in a high room—make it seem lower.

Vertical lines in a room—make it appear lower.

A scenic paper with a third dimension—adds perspective and creates the illusion of space.

A dark paint on the ceiling or wallpaper coming down on the wall—makes a ceiling appear lower.

Large patterns—make furniture appear more prominent and decrease the apparent size of the room.

Pine paneling laid horizontally—gives a spacious and sturdy effect, especially when wide boards and shallow heading are used.

A high ceiling—gives a room a feeling of spaciousness.

Mirrors—add to a feeling of spaciousness.

Natural wood—presents a neutral appearance.

Ceiling slope down toward the window walls—enhances the intimate coziness of the room.

A darkened room—sets a mellow mood.

Foil paper—dramatizes a high ceiling and makes it an important part of the room.

Plain neutral backgrounds—expand space and create a restful atmosphere.

Fitted carpets and timber-covered walls and ceiling—give the room a comfortable atmosphere.

Lines—define decorative and architectural elements.

Walls lined with books—make a most effective, lively decoration.

White and earth colors—contribute to the atmosphere of cool spaciousness.

A few notable paintings and sculptures, plus books and accessories—increase the feeling of vibrancy while adding points of interest.

Skylights—always add a lively feeling to space.

A sparsely furnished area, planned with sensitivity to form and texture—becomes quite spacious.

When all areas are visible to the eye at one time—the space appears larger than it really is.

Niches into walls, arches, alcoves, window openings, and recessed lamps, television, and sound equipment—create super space-age environment.

Fur, real and fake—provides a guaranteed status interior.

Gold foil wallpaper, yellow enamel buffet, and Icelandic sheepskin floor covering—make a room conjure up the Hollywood interior for exponents of the "star system."

Use of natural materials—makes strong colors unnecessary.

Color and exceptionally handsome furniture—enliven a calm and peaceful living room.

SPACE EVALUATION EXERCISES

Objectives and Procedures

Although in actual practice one would normally be interested in evaluating a recently designed and built space, for demonstration purposes any complex space might serve—a remote computing room, a library reference room, a bookstore, or a large lounge. One is interested in how well the space "works" from two principal standpoints. First, what sort of effectiveness do various design approaches and features have as a basis for future designs? Second, if there are defects in this space, what are they and how should they be corrected—both in a short-term, low-cost "fix" and in a longer-term, higher-priced redo? These general objectives should be kept in mind in both the evaluation and its reporting.

Each of the design/evaluation criteria—health/safety, performance, comfort, and pleasantness—is always appropriate to some degree. However, from space to space, the relative importance of the criteria will vary considerably, which may reflect the values of the client. A college administrator might say that he isn't concerned with the pleasantness of the classroom. The nature of the space might set priorities: serious safety and performance problems might dictate inattention to other design aspects. The same observations may be appropriate to several criteria—temperature measures, for example. Rather moderate deviations from the optimum, however, may make this a comfort problem rather than a health or performance problem.

Although a team of evaluators can carry out the evaluation faster, the evaluation can all be done by one person. Again, most of the procedures are straightforward, requiring little special training or familiarity with special instruments. If there is any possibility of air contamination or radiation, a specialist should be employed to assess this health hazard.

Steps

Subjective Impression. Even though you may have been in the space a number of times, visit it. Spend a few minutes observing the space. How does it grab you? Write down your reactions!

Executive Interview. Arrange to talk to at least one person in a position of responsibility with respect to the space. Tell him your objectives and intended activities. Ask him for cooperation. Offer to provide feedback in the form of your report. Ask him for any thoughts he has about the space. These should include what the space is intended for and how well he feels it does these things.

User Interview. Seek out one or more users of the space. Interview him about the space. Start with general questions and probe into specific areas—features that are desirable or undesirable.

User Questionnaire. In broadest terms the objectives of the questionnaire should get at user feelings of aesthetic pleasantness, comfort, and user beliefs about how well people can perform the intended functions in the space. (It is also conceivable in certain cases that user beliefs about how well people can perform the intended functions in the space. (It is also conceivable in certain cases that user beliefs about health and safety aspects of the space should be solicited.)

Use the results from the interviews as a partial guide. Construct a brief questionnaire asking questions about important aspects of the several design criteria.

In the case of pleasantness there should be questions relating to a general evaluation dimension and to whatever other dimensions you think relevant to the space. An aesthetic pleasantness scale follows. For example, a relaxing dimension would be appropriate for a student lounge.

For comfort or discomfort include whatever features are relevant. Normally they would include at least lighting, noise, thermal, and seating features.

For performance, each important task should be assessed.

Measurements. In a large space, sample a number of positions, measuring illumination, sound level, temperature, and humidity. If there are any specific conditions that would lead to large variations in conditions, make additional readings. For instance, if light fixtures are widely spaced or if there are a number of different light sources, including windows, measure to determine these effects. Similarly, if there are significant contributers to the noise level or to the heat or cold, measure to assess their impact. If a photometer is available, measure the luminance of light sources and their surroundings and other important room surfaces. Sample different times of day when different natural lighting or temperature effects might vary or when people or machine activity variations might have an impact.

Relate these measures to comfort criteria. If these are exceeded, consider the possibility of performance or health effects.

Performance Observations. By observing personnel at workstations and/or performing or simulating performance at workstations yourself (on a noninterference basis) attempt to judge the adequacy of displays, controls, arrangement, lighting, seating, and the like for performing at the station. Obtain illumination readings at each work level and compare to requirements.

Observe the flow of people and materials into, out of, and within the facility. As deemed necessary and practicable, tabulate movements. Make any tables or diagrams desirable to portray situation.

Safety checklist. In the box following is a checklist, which should be reviewed for the space. In addition, the space should be generally examined for hazards, with an observation of activities of the occupants for hazardous practices associated with the space. Finally, if the space is a manufacturing facility or involves any complex machinery or hazardous operations, a specialist should carry out a safety inspection.

SAFETY CHECKLIST

Walking-Working Surfaces
All walkways are properly marked and cleared.
All floor holes, floor openings, wall openings, and skylights are properly guarded.
Nonslip mats, gratings, false floors, and other like materials are in use in wet and other hazardous areas.
All floor surfaces are in good repair.
All open-sided floors, platforms, and runways 4 feet or more above ground or floor level are properly guarded with toe boards and railings installed.

Stairs and Stairways
All stairways and elevated and escalator shafts are clear, handrails and/or guardrails provided, and treads and risers are in good repair with nonslip surfaces and adequate illumination.

Ventilation
All work areas appear to be properly ventilated with no accumulation of smoke, dust, or other hazardous material noted.

Lane Safety
Location and easy accessibility of at least two fire-emergency exits for each work area confirmed, with special attention to high-hazard areas.
Each fire emergency exit is marked and illuminated.
The route to safety is clear and unobstructed.
All emergency doors swing in the direction of exit travel.
Emergency doors cannot be locked to the inside; each is equipped with panic or other simple type of releasing device.
All portable fire extinguishers are readily accessible and properly located and show servicing is up-to-date; maximum travel distance for all units is not in excess of 75 feet, or 50 feet in hazardous areas.
All fire hoses appear to be in good condition.

Where manual fire alarm boxes are used, each is accessible from maximum travel distance of 200 feet, with the travel path unencumbered.

Electrical Wiring, Apparatus, and Equipment
Extension cords and other temporary wiring do not have breaks, fraying, or other defects.
Electrical equipment operating between 50 and 600 volts is protected against accidental contact by enclosures.
Each electrical outlet box is provided with a cover that effectively protects the hazard from accidental contact.

Machine Guarding and Mechanical Safety
Every machine has been inspected as to the following items and found to be in satisfactory operating condition:

a. Cleanliness of machine and area
b. Secure attachment to floor
c. Guarded operations
d. Illumination
e. Effective cut-off devices
f. Noise level
g. Adjustment
h. Material flow

Material Storage
All material is stored in such a way that it does not create either a fire hazard or a safety hazard to personnel.

Seating and Furniture Comfort. For each different seat and work position, have several judges sit in it for five minutes and then make judgments on the following scale:

Uncomfortable			So-So		Comfortable	
1	2	3	4	5	6	7

For any judgments of "1," "2," or "3" obtain a further response as to why this judgment was made (such as pressure on calves, thighs, back, no place to put feet, arms).

Pleasantness Ratings. Using either regular users or others or both, follow these procedures, using the accompanying scales to rate dimensions of pleasantness.

1. Each judge should make all ratings of spaces independent of others' opinions on the scales provided.

2. Determine the median rating over judges for each pair of terms (scale). The median is the middle score. Thus if there were five scores, say, 2, 2, 3, 5, 7, the median would be "3." If there are an even number of scores, the median is halfway between the middle two. If there were four scores, say, 2, 3, 6, 7, the median would be 4.5.

3. Add the three medians for "E" (evaluation), that is, "interesting," "pleasant," and "beautiful." Divide this sum by three. Do the same for the three medians for "O" (orderliness) and "S" (spaciousness).

4. Consider any rating between 3 and 5 "average," above 5 "high," and below 3 "low."

Now how do the characteristics that you earlier listed seem to relate to these ratings?

				Average			
(E)	Interesting						Uninteresting
	7	6	5	4	3	2	1
(O)	Disorderly			Average			Orderly
	1	2	3	4	5	6	7
(S)	Roomy			Average			Not Roomy
	7	6	5	4	3	2	1
(E)	Unpleasant			Average			Pleasant
	1	2	3	4	5	6	7
(O)	Neat			Average			Messy
	7	6	5	4	3	2	1
(S)	Crowded			Average			Spacious
	1	2	3	4	5	6	7
(E)	Beautiful			Average			Ugly
	7	6	5	4	3	2	1
(O)	Untidy			Average			Tidy
	1	2	3	4	5	6	7
(S)	Uncluttered			Average			Cluttered
	7	6	5	4	3	2	1

REFERENCES

Bennett, C. A., and P. Rey. What's so hot about red? *Human Factors,* 14(2): 145-150, 1972.

Canter, David V. (ed.). *Architectural psychology—Proceedings of the conference at the University of Strathclyde.* London: RIBA Publications Limited, 1970.

Hill, A. R. Visibility and privacy. In D. V. Canter, (ed.). *Architectural psychology.* London: RIBA, 1970.

Keck, M. E. Batting performance for day vs. night baseball games. *Illuminating Engineering,* 65(10): 590-593, 1970.

Kilty, T. K. The readability of commonly encountered materials. *Human Factors Society Bulletin,* 19(7):3-4, 1976.

Parsons, H. W. What happened at Hawthorne? *Science,* 183: 922-932, 1974.

Payne, J. Pupillary responses to architectural stimuli. In D. V. Canter (ed.). *Architectural psychology.* London: RIBA, 1970.

Payne, S. L. *The art of asking questions.* Princeton, New Jersey: Princeton University Press, 1951.

Sommer, R. *Personal space: The behavioral basis of design.* Englewood Cliffs, N. J.: Prentice-Hall, 1969.

Walters, D. Annoyance due to railway noise in residential areas. In D. V. Carter, (ed.). *Architectural psychology.* London: RIBA, 1970.

Webb, E. J., D. T. Campbell, R. D. Schwartz, and L. Sechrest. *Unobtrusive Measures: Nonreactive research in the social sciences.* Chicago: Rand-McNally, 1966.

Weixelman, J. J. Sign size and location and attention getting. Unpublished report. Kansas State University. 1973.

Wools, R. M. The assessment of room friendliness. In D. V. Canter, (ed.). *Architectural psychology.* London: RIBA, 1970.

10

Creativity and Problem-Solving

"There is nothing more fearful than imagination without taste."

GOETHE

A designer should be a creative problem-solver. People who are more creative tend to be independent and intelligent. Various stages in the problem-solving process have been identified. Recommendations for problem-solving and creativity are described.

A designer should be a creative problem-solver.

A designer should be a creative problem-solver. What does that mean? How are creativity and problem-solving different? Look at Figure 10.1 The upper part of the figure shows that where a problem exists there may be a number of possible solutions. This is "creativity." The lower part of the figure shows that where a problem exists, a number of considerations, pieces of information, or constraints exist. These limit the "solutions" that actually solve the problem. "Design a capitol building for the new nation of Rurathenia." This calls for creativity. "The new capitol building must serve certain specific government functions, meld with the local architecture,

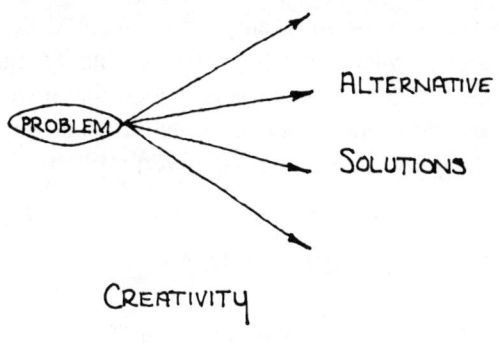

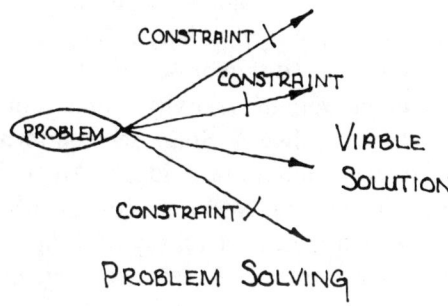

Figure 10.1 *Creativity and problem solving.*

cost less than. . . ." This calls for problem-solving. As the example suggests, real cases call for both creativity and problem-solving. At times in the discussion either creativity or problem-solving will be emphasized. It has sometimes been noted that in industry creative people are not always prized. The creative person may say, "If we did this, then so and so. If we did that, then such and such." The industrial (and other organizational) manager's reaction may be, "My problem is this. How do I solve it? I'm not really concerned with so-and-so or such-and-such. Ideas are cheap. What I need is solutions to my (present) problems." The other term to be mentioned is "originality." Being original means being different. A contemporary artist may emphasize being different. A designer, who may also value originality, must be concerned that her work is practical, that it works. That is the difference between creativity and originality. A designer should be a creative problem-solver.

INDIVIDUAL DIFFERENCES

As in everything else, people differ in creativity—only more so. The writer and his colleagues (Bennett *et al.*, 1969) carried out an experiment to test the effectiveness of various techniques intended to make people more creative (more on it later). The really impressive result was how different—regardless of techniques—the people were in creativity. Some people had a lot of good ideas, always. Some seemed to have only a few rather commonplace ideas. Most of us have noticed this variability in our acquaintances. A Frank Lloyd Wright with a vast array of design ideas is extremely rare. Most of us are so-so in creativity. Some people seem rarely to come up with anything new.

As children, creative people were distinct.

The question is, "Why?" Why are some so creative and some not? Work by California psychologists Mackinon and Barron (Barron, 1958, 1965, 1969) and others suggests that as a child, the more creative person had more creative hobbies, was more solitary, more independent, more nonconventional, had strong drives, tended to be unhappy, rebelled against his teachers, and believed in his own work. These traits also tend to characterize adult creative people.

The more creative person is different in many ways.

What the Berkeley group did was to ask people in various fields—mathematics, architecture, writing, and so on—to identify those in the field who were especially creative. Those people who appeared on a number of such lists were considered creative. They were invited to California for a few days. Then people in the same field who were considered competent but not especially creative were also invited. Psychologists—unaware of who was who—talked with these people and tested them. The more creative tended to prefer more complex, asymmetrical designs and complex messy drawings to neat simple ones. They had good senses of humor, were unconventional in their aspirations, and were more like psychologists, architects, and authors in their interests than they were like bankers, farmers, and salesmen. The creative individual was found to be unconventional, "courted the irrational in himself," was observant, vigorous, interested in the truth, and led a complex life.

Is the creative person "crazy," as some popular belief holds? Not necessarily, but he is not conventional; he may be eccentric. As in any other group, some creative people are psychotic. Is the creative person highly intelligent? Again, not necessarily. Some evidence suggests that up to an IQ of about 120 (the average for college graduates), creativity increases with intelligence. Beyond that level of intelligence, there seems to be no correlation with creativity. It seems that a certain minimal intelligence is needed to be creative. Writers, among the highly creative, are the most intelligent. But then intelligence tests are highly verbal, while other aptitudes are presumably crucial in fields like mathematics and architecture. In general, although there were some such differences among the various groups of creative people, they were similar.

Creative people tend to be similar and intelligent.

A BRIEF CREATIVITY TEST

A 15-item creativity test was constructed from a larger set of questions used to assess creativity in the California studies by Berkeley psychologist Harrison Gough (Wernick, 1955). As no norms exist for this test, there is no way to say whether one is "very creative" or not. However, it might be interesting to answer the questions and then look at the scoring key at the end of the chapter that tells you how most creative people answered each item.

1. T (F) Once I have made up my mind about something, I seldom change it.
2. T (F) I am very careful about my manner of dress.
3. T (F) I am often so annoyed when someone tries to get ahead of me in a line of people that I speak to him about it.
4. T (F) I always follow the rule: business before pleasure.
5. T (F) Compared to my own self-respect, the respect of others means little.
6. (T) F At times I have been so entertained by the cleverness of a crook that I have hoped that he would get by with it.
7. T (F) I don't like to work on a problem unless there is a possibility of coming out with a clear-cut and unambiguous answer.
8. T (F) I commonly wonder what hidden reason another person may have for doing something nice for me.
9. (T) F Sometimes I rather enjoy going against the rules and doing things I am not supposed to.
10. (T) F I like to fool around with new ideas, even if they turn out later to be a total waste of time.
11. T (F) I get annoyed with writers who go out of their way to use strange and unusual words.
12. T (F) For most questions, there is just one right answer, once a person is able to get the facts.
13. (T) F I would like the job of foreign correspondent for a newspaper.
14. (T) F Every boy ought to get away from his family for a year or two while he is still in his teens.
15. T (F) The trouble with many people is that they don't take things seriously enough.

PHASES IN CREATIVITY AND PROBLEM SOLVING

Although some formal research has been done on what happens during the creative or problem-solving process, much of our understanding is strongly influenced by self-reflection and by analysis of and by creative people.

General Preparation

Before getting concerned with a particular problem, the problem-solver needs to become generally prepared in the subject matter. Although education may usually have a negative effect on creativity—because of its emphasis on the exposition of common solutions to problems, learning rote procedures to solve problems, and sometimes negative reinforcement of creative behavior—some training in English, mathematics, or what have you is needed. It's hard to be a creative architect unless one is an architect. John Lowes (1927), in his magnificent book about the English writer Samuel Coleridge, shows in great detail how Coleridge's reading of the books of his time was a crucial basis for his famous *Rhyme of the Ancient Mariner*.

You need to know something to be creative.

Problem Recognition

Sometimes the problem is given. "The problem is to . . . ." In most practical situations, a problem reformulation, at least, is critical. "Maybe, if the arrangement of offices in accordance with work flow is unsatisfactory because the work flow is continually changing and rearrangements cost money, the problem is to avoid rearrangement rather than to accommodate the work flow. Perhaps we should use an arbitrary or random arrangement." In the extreme case—perhaps the most significant case—it is the problem recognition that counts. There is the famous case of Becquerel, who found the photo plates in his laboratory fogged up and thereby discovered the radioactivity of uranium. Perhaps there were photo plates fogged up in

Knowing the problem can sometimes be the solution.

laboratories all over the world, but only Becquerel recognized that this might mean something important.

Information Gathering

Get the facts!

The problem has been formulated. Now comes a period of amassing information. If the interior of the embassy at Rurathenia is to be designed, then a lot of information about embassies should be gotten, and some about Rurathenia. This information must be studied and assimilated as well as forming reference material. This is part of the perspiration of inspiration.

Generation of Alternative Solutions

Try!

Now that a lot is known about the problem and related matters, alternative solutions are generated. In the complex case of interior design, there may be several stages, including floor planning and decorating, as the designer goes through the various steps of designing. Hopefully, at each stage, a satisfactory solution will result. If it doesn't, then further steps are needed.

Incubation

If at first you don't succeed, wait!

If a continuous period of active problem-solving doesn't give satisfactory results, but the thinker hasn't given up, an incubation period takes place. What happens during incubation? Apparently, nothing. Nothing visible or within awareness, at least. The problem-solver puts the problem aside and does other work. Two things may happen regarding the problem. First, it may be that the person is actually thinking about the problem out of his awareness ("unconsciously"). A second possibility is that really nothing is happening but that the thinker forgets harmful "sets" or habitual ways of thinking about the problem—ways that were keeping him from solving the problem. When those sets are dissipated, the problem-solver may have an illumination.

Illumination / Solution Selection

An illumination, an inspiration, a "light-bulb-lighting," is that happy occurence of a solution or creative thought. This can be quite dramatic—a sudden happening in the midst of some other activity. The creativity literature contains many examples of this. While working on my master's thesis, I suddenly got the solution to a minor mathematical problem that had been stumping me as I stepped off the bus one day, thinking about something unrelated. Coleridge, who was a drug addict, awoke from a drugged stupor and started writing *Kubla Khan*—it just rushed forth from the dream he had had. Unfortunately, someone interrupted Coleridge for an hour or so, and he was never able to finish this remarkable poem.

An illumination can be a sudden, dramatic solution.

Many times a dramatic inspiration doesn't take place. Rather, a number of "reasonable" solutions have been generated. These must be examined to select the best. Sometimes this process will be subjective or intuitive. That is, we just "look them over and pick the best." Sometimes some analytical evaluation technique will be helpful, such as was described for floor planning. More and more mathematical techniques ("optimization," "operations research") are being developed for this purpose. Sometimes these techniques merely verify what the decision-maker already knew.

A best solution may be selected.

Verification or Evaluation

Verification or evaluation is the review of the solution to see if it is satisfactory. Although some might feel

Verification is seeing if the solution works.

that this is not a part of the creative process, if it leads to going back and trying again, verification is clearly relevant.

TECHNIQUES FOR IMPROVING CREATIVITY

Approaches to the Process

Research in creativity is needed.

As creativity is highly prized in some circles, there has been considerable interest in ways to improve it. A number of creativity-training programs have been developed and a number sold to industries. Although several small fortunes have probably been made, there appears to be little evidence of the usefulness of creativity training. Some evaluation research has been done, but it has tended to be flawed by serious methodological problems like improper control groups and creativity tests that look a lot like the creativity-training exercises. Based on the literature, some recommendations for being more creative can be made. There are also some "creativity techniques" intended to help generate solutions. Although these seem plausible, unfortunately there is little evidence that they are valid.

Study!

Certainly, study is called for as general preparation. Some of this may be formal training, some self-study of designs, materials, hardware, and what have you. Unfortunately, formal professional training, as well as being necessary, probably stifles creativity as well. As an example, in the training of research psychologists, the following trend can be noted: Undergraduate students have a lot of interesting ideas to do research on but generally don't know how to design methodologically sound studies. Graduate students still have some original ideas, although more of their research ideas fit into existing molds of research. Graduate instruction, of course, emphasizes how to do

There seems to be an inverse relation between a professional approach and creativity.

studies, not what. By the time we come to mature professional psychologists, practically all the research is on well-studied problems, but very well executed. Similar things happen in the training of designers. One way this has been put is, "They design for their colleagues rather than their clients."

A further step in the study process is to keep track of interesting ideas one sees and ideas one has. Creative people keep notebooks or files.

Problem recognition can probably be improved if one can learn to be more critical. "Why doesn't this work? "Is that really the problem?" Probably this is like noticing you have a "slice" (bias to the right) in golf. What do you do about it? Perhaps simply develop a habit in problem situations of *always* questioning the apparent situation.

Question the problem!

Information gathering, for some, can be improved simply by doing more of it. Others do too much—not directly, but because extended information gathering can be an excuse for not trying to solve the problem. Because the thinker fears failure at problem solving, he delays engaging in it.

Prepare, but don't waste time at it!

Some experimentation has been done on actually getting solutions. Vinacke (1952) reports a study by Eindhoven who compared how artists and nonartists drew pictures to fit a poem. The artists made a lot of preliminary sketches, quickly trying out a lot of ideas. Once they had selected one they spent a lot of time developing it. Non-artists made a drawing, spent a lot of time developing it, then made another and developed it, and so on.

Try a lot of ideas without wasting time, before doing detailed design!

Finally, "go back to the well." A UCLA psychologist, Maltzman (1958), has shown experimentally that by forcing the problem-solver to try and try again for new and better solutions, some new and better solutions will come.

Try again!

The best thing you can do about incubation is to allow time for it. If project planning gets the job

Allow time for incubation!

started early enough and confines the active information gathering and solution generation, then there will be time to put the job aside for incubation. When you come back you may have a better idea. The same statements apply to verification; the more time you allow yourself before you must conclude your design with verification, the more likely you will be to detect a design flaw. You may not like this idea of controlling the time of your creative activity, but ultimately you will have to do this; you will have to get the job done sometime. You *can* create on schedule. You'll be surprised at what you can do. One of the principal benefits of the deadline is that it forces you to stop time-wasting activities and get down to business. A similar beneficial action is to set a time and a place for creativity: "Every morning I go into the garden for 10 minutes to think." The advantage is that one develops a habitual activity where the likelihood of interference by irrelevancies is minimized.

Operational Techniques

Several techniques for generating ideas exist.

A number of techniques have been devised to help people generate ideas that might be creative in response to some problem. Two of these—brainstorming and synectics—are generally thought of as group techniques, but they could be adopted as idea-generating techniques for a person working by himself. See how the techniques might be used, consider these problems: A designer wishes to devise a new office desk. Problem: How can a conventional desk be changed? Or: A designer would like to modify a private office. Problem: How can a private office be changed?

Checklists.

Checklists. Osborne (1950) has suggested a checklist of modifications the designer might use, for example, adapt, modify, magnify, minify, cheapen, improve quality, multiply, omit, divide, substitute, rearrange, reverse, combine. The desk designer considers each modifier to see if any worthy changes are found. For example, "Magnify—suppose I enlarged the desk to fill the entire office, encompassing all its functions—the desk becomes the office." Or, "Substitute—I might substitute carpet for the metal or wood surface of a desk." And so on.

Attribute Listing. Crawford (Osborne, 1950) has suggested listing the various attributes of the item that are of interest, then asking how each could be changed. The office is rectilinear—it could be made curved or irregular. It may be large—it could be made small like a Pullman compartment. It is electrically lighted—it might be given a substantial skylight. The office is quiet—it might have background music. And so on.

Attributes.

Focused Object. Whiting (1958) has devised an interesting technique he called "focused object." Here, in order to modify the desk, another item is selected. By randomly looking in the Sears catalog or a dictionary or somewhere, an unrelated thing is selected, say a Selectric Typewriter. The characteristics of this item are examined to see if they could be applied to the desk. For instance, the desk could be electrified. The selectric has a print ball which can be changed for the occasion. Could the contents—papers—of the desk be containerized and switched depending on the worker's current job? The typewriter comes in a variety of colors. The typewriter has been "styled." And so on.

A random object is selected.

Brainstorming. Even though brainstorming is generally thought of as a group technique, an individual could apply (and generally should, regardless of technique) the "reserved judgment" feature. In

Reserve judgment!

brainstorming sessions the group is asked to contribute ideas—whatever occurs to them—without thought for their goodness. The group is to reserve judgment on the goodness of others' ideas. Brainstorming is a technique for *generating* ideas, and the ideas can be evaluated later. This aspect of brainstorming is crucial. Without reserved judgment, a brainstorming session is just a group discussion of the problem. Probably the other important feature of the method is a display of the group's ideas, say a listing on a blackboard; previous ideas can stimulate new ones.

Abstract brainstorming.

Synectics. This again is a group idea-generation scheme. But whereas in brainstorming the group might focus on the actual problem—campus parking, for example—in synectics perhaps only the group leader knows that parking is the problem. He presents a more abstract problem, "storage." The group then brainstorms storage ("How do bees store honey?"). Later these ideas can be related to parking. This method may avoid stereotyped responses to the problem.

Try it! You may like it.

Comment. As indicated, there isn't evidence that the techniques work. The writer and his colleagues (1969) compared three individual idea-generators with a no-technique condition and found that if anything, the techniques interfered with idea generation. Taylor, as described by Whiting (1958), compared group brainstorming with the ideas that the same number of people generated working alone. Substantially more ideas were generated by individual thinkers. Both of these studies suffered from problem-solving time limitations—it takes some time to apply the techniques. Group brainstorming with an existing group may have the additional benefit of commitment. If a group of executives brainstormed the topic, "how to improve sales of product L," they might more likely feel that whatever resulted was a good approach. The designer is advised to try the techniques for herself. If they seem to help, use them!

DISCUSSION

If one set a premium on creativity, could he do things to make himself more creative? What could he do? Would behaving more independently and eccentrically be worthwhile?

GENERATING IDEAS

Take some design problem, for instance, how to decorate a classroom in a way that would be appealing, inexpensive, and lasting. (You might question the final criterion.) Let each person first work individually: Simply think of all the solutions you can. Write these down. Then, in turn, try the checklist, attribute-listing, and focused-object techniques, each time writing them down, identifying the technique, and trying to add to the previous ideas. Now form a group and brainstorm. Feel free to suggest your previously thought-up ideas as they may stimulate further ideas. Have someone write down the ideas for all to see. Now individually, go back and analyze what happened with each method of generating ideas. Comment on the value of each approach.

REFERENCES

BARRON, F. The psychology of imagination. *Scientific American,* 199(3):150-166, 1958.

BARRON, F. The psychology of creativity. In *New directions in psychology II*. New York: Holt, Rinehart and Winston, 1965.

BARRON, F. *Creative person and creative process*. New York: Holt, Rinehart and Winston, 1969.

BENNETT, C. A., K. T. TIMMS, and T. B. SPRECHER. *An experimental comparison of several problem-solving techniques.* Paper presented at the 40th Annual Meeting of the Eastern Psychological Association, Philadelphia, April 1969.

LOWES, J. L. *The road to Xanadu.* Boston: Houghton, Mifflin, 1927.

MALTZMAN, I., W. BOGARTZ, and L. BREGER. A procedure for increasing word association originality and its transfer effects. *Journal of Experimental Psychology,* 56:392-398, 1958.

OSBORN, A. *Applied imagination.* New York: Scribners, 1950.

VINACKE, W. E. *The psychology of thinking.* New York: McGraw-Hill, 1952.

WERNICK, R. Modern-style mind reader. *Life,* 39(11), 97-108, 1955.

WHITING, C. S. *Creative thinking.* New York: Reinhold, 1958.

Creative Test Key

1. F	2. F	3. T	4. F	5. T	6. T	7. F
8. F	9. T	10. T	11. F	12. F	13. T	14. T
15. F						

11

Presenting the Design

"In seminars and arenas the difference between being bored and being gored is the quality of the bull."

J. A. PERKINS.

A good design is insufficient; it must be sold. The key design features should be related to the clients' motives. A theme should be developed. The predesign analysis and the design must be communicated to a layman. Key points should be summarized and the presentation practiced.

As in many walks of life it is not enough to do a good (design) job; others must know you have done a good job. You must communicate your work—your design—to the client. You must convince him that it is good; you must sell him on it.

You must communicate and sell your design.

Although you might, especially with large jobs, be called on to make a written presentation, the oral presentation is more common and generally more important. This presentation may occur at various stages in the design. It may be rather informal—merely chatting with the client—or it may be a formal stand-up presentation to a group representing the client. In any case, you should formally prepare to communicate and sell your work.

Formal preparation is crucial.

Read a book, take a course.

Many good books have been written on oral communication. One of these is by Fotheringham (1966). Many courses are given. The designer should seriously consider further study of this topic.

PLAN

Leave time to prepare your presentation.

Time is generally in short supply. Usually there won't be enough time to do the design job the way you would like. The tendency is to use all of your available time in designing—after all, you are a designer—with no time left for preparing your pitch. However, you must plan your work, leaving enough time for presentation planning. It will count a lot in how well your design is received.

Plan in order to present a complex design.

Another common error is to assume that because you are the designer and thus understand your design very well, you can automatically present it in an understandable fashion. These are two separate tasks. Only a few brilliant people can make a sensible presentation of a complex subject without a plan for presentation.

MOTIVES AND MEMORY

List the client's motives and your design's features.

You can make a better presentation if you keep in mind that the major object is not to present your design but to show how your design satisfies the client's motives or needs. Start by making a list. List all the things the client said or seemed to want in the design. (Of course, you also did this before designing.) For example, he said he wanted a lobby that would impress the visitors with the importance of the company, as a lot of selling is done there. Also list all the good features of the design; mention all the good things it does. Your choice of modular office workplace units with their own partitions will provide flexibility, permitting easy and inexpensive rearrangement as the client's firm grows. Some of your key design features will fit motives the client "didn't even know he had." That's okay. You're the designer, an expert. You know things the client doesn't know. If you programmed well you know what he wants and what he needs.

Now you need to organize the motives and features into a presentation. First, select the motive-feature that you think is most important to the customer. In many cases the fact that your design does this one thing is sufficient. Generally, unless the client —usually some executive—is particularly sensitive to the functionality of the design, the principal motive you can satisfy is that "it looks good." This may not be the motive-feature to emphasize in your presentation. If the design appeals to the client aesthetically, it will influence him whether he knows it or not. It won't hurt to point out how beautiful your design is. However, you may want to call attention to some functional, money-saving feature. Generally, the client must justify buying the design to someone else or to himself. If he can say, "Because of the greater density of an open-plan design, we are going to save a lot of money," all else may be unimportant. Usually, satisfying that one important motive will sell the design. It will be important, however, to present a number of motive-features. If you can't be sure of your target, you shoot a shotgun. You may want to avoid presenting too many motive-features at first; keep some in reserve, and don't confuse the client.

Select the important motive-features.

The motive-features should be organized into an overall theme, one idea emphasized to tie the motive-features together. The purpose of the theme is organization, so that the client can remember the various features. Not only are you trying to communicate and sell, but you want the client to be able to sell your

Select a theme to help the client remember the design features.

design himself—to others and to himself. As an example, "The theme of this design is SPACE. (1) The space has been organized to obtain good workflow. (2) Space has been used to provide needed privacy. (3) The choice of design elements has been made to provide feelings of spaciousness. PROPER USE OF SPACE—ORGANIZATION, PRIVACY, AND FEELINGS.

THE DESIGN

The introductory material of your presentation summarized the important features of the design. Now the design must be communicated in some detail.

Analyses will show the client how the design fits.

Just as you did various analyses as a basis for design, such as floor planning, you should present the analyses to the client. You want to accomplish two ends: First, you want to show him that you have studied his problem as a basis for design. Second, you want to show him further—now in some detail—how your design meets his needs. The tendency, however, is to give him too much detail, although some feel that there is an advantage in deliberately "snowing" the client. Generally, you should reduce the analytic detail to a level you believe he is interested in and capable of absorbing. It's like a parent answering a child's question about sex—the child is not as interested as the parent is. Keep it brief. Time may also be a factor. At least show the client a simplified diagram of how his business will be conducted in the designed space, again showing how well the design fits. Whatever the client's priorities, the analysis will help him rationalize cost and help him convince others. Cost rationalization is crucial in our culture.

The overall nature of the design should be shown first, and the detailed exposition should wait. Visuals or graphics are, of course, the key to communicating the design. What may be easy for the designer bending over her board to understand may be impossible for the client. Spatial visualization is like mathematics—many otherwise highly intelligent people are dumbbells at it. Several suggestions are in order: Keep the graphics as simple as possible. Present only features which the client cares about. Put less important details on separate drawings or make them inconspicuous. Make delineation obvious. Use high contrast linework and use a large scale. Do *not* assume that people can understand floor plans. Use isometrics or, better, perspectives or, better, models or perhaps slides of models. The easier-to-understand representations are, of course, more expensive. They will be worth the cost if they enable the client to understand a good design. They also, of course, can help you, the designer, to visualize during the design process. Some aspects of design, such as lighting, are practically impossible to represent except by models.

The problem is how to communicate the design.

SUMMARY AND REHEARSAL

Finally, you must summarize. Summarize the motives, the analysis, the key features of the design, the theme. Be repetitive. You want the client to remember the good things you are telling him.

Summarize!

Rehearse. Again few people can give a complex presentation well without practice. It may be difficult to turn yourself into a super pitchman. You can avoid being a lousy one, by planning and practice. Use as detailed a set of notes as you need. Know what you will say by having said it. Tape record and listen to it. Get someone to listen and critique. Make you presentation as formally as you will with the client. Check the time against the time you expect to have—go under, not over that limit. Watch your manner. Be

Rehearse!

interested—show that your design is interesting. You did a good design, now sell it.

DISCUSSION

How (better) can various aspects of design be represented—the floor plan, the view, the decor, the lighting, the furnishings, the privacy, the spaciousness?

REPRESENTATION

Consider your current or most recent design project. List the key design features, that is, the features that you felt made it better than average. Now do two things: (1) Write a brief pitch relating them to the client (hypothetical, if necessary) and his motives. (2) Create a different means of representing at least one of these features so that the client can better understand it.

REFERENCE

FOTHERINGHAM, W. C. *Perspectives on persuasion.* Boston: Allyn and Bacon, 1966.

Index

A

accidents, 5, 12, 13
activities, (*see* Layout, functional)
activity, 18, 19, 127, 133, 135, 157
actualization, 20
aesthetic pleasantness (*see* Pleasantness)
age effects, 28, 46, 87, 91 (*see also* Presbyopia, Presbycousis)
air velocity, 127, 128, 132, 135
Allen, E.C., 110
Allport, Gordon, 150
American Society of Heating, Refrigeration and Air Conditioning Engineers (ASHRAE), 132
analytical evaluation, 9, 82
animals, 59–60
annoyance from noise, 113, 122–124, 125, 144
anthropometry, 6, 25, 27–32, 34, 59
anxiety, 121
architecture, 4, 64, 164, 165, 167
arm rests, 41
attribute listing, 173
Ayoub, M.M., 36, 57

B

back, 15, 35, 36, 37, 38
barriers, 58, 61, 64, 65, 66, 141
Barron, Frank, 164, 175
bars (*see* Restaurants and bars)
Becquerel, 167
bedrooms, 58, 64, 101, 123, 133, 145, 151
Bennett, Corwin A., 3, 11, 17, 22, 38, 43, 46, 64, 161, 164, 174, 176
Beranek, L.L., 122, 126
Berenson, P.J., 130, 136
Blackwell, H. Richard, 92, 110
Bogartz, W., 176
brainstorming, 173–174, 175
Breger, L., 132
brightness (*see* Luminance)
Brookes, Malcolm, 29, 57
building code, 12
built environment, 3, 5, 6, 18
Buttolf, L.J., 46, 57

C

CIE (International Commission on Lighting), 93
Campbell, D.T., 161
Canter, David V., 10, 141, 161
Chaplin, Charlie, 66
checklists, for creativity, 172–173
Chidsey, K.D., 57
Chitlangia, Anand, 93, 110
chroma (*see* Saturation)
classrooms and schools, 3, 4, 7, 28, 65, 72, 73–75, 120, 123, 124, 125, 145, 155
client, 146, 177–182
closeness-desired relations, 69, 72–75, 76, 81
clothing, 127, 128, 133, 135
Cogan, D.G., 89, 110
cold (*see* Heat and cold)
Coleridge, Samuel Taylor, 167, 169

Collins, J.B., 16, 23
color, 104–109, 154, 155
color harmony, 7, 107–108
color warmth, 87, 106, 108, 109, 139-141
color pleasantness, 87, 106–108
comfort, 1, 7, 8, 11, 12, 13, 14–16, 21, 27, 45, 48, 52, 82, 85, 89, 155, 156, 157 (*see also* Seat comfort, Thermal comfort)
computers, 69, 79-82, 153
conduction, 128
confounding, 146
contamination, 5, 6, 12, 85, 156, 158
contrast, 87, 91, 92, 98, 101, 102, 107
convection, 128
convenience, 14, 53
CORELAP, 81–82
Corlett, E.N., 16, 22
correlational research, 143–144
Crawford, 173
creativity and problem solving, 8–9, 11, 65, 137, 162–176
creativity techniques, 170–175
creativity test, 165–166
critical task concept, 92, 95
Crouch, Cazimer L., 46, 57, 89, 110
crowding, 59–60, 131

D

daylight, 89
defensive seating (*see* Face the action)
Department of Labor, 12, 22
design complexity and specialization, 3–5, 11
design team, 4
design theory, 16
design and evaluation criteria, 1, 7, 8, 11–23, 82, 87, 104, 128, 153, 155–156, 157
design hierarchy, 11–12, 13, 19, 20
design-evaluation cycle, 8-9
detail size, 87
disability glare effects, 87, 98

discomfort (*see* Comfort)
discomfort (glare) effects, 87, 98–102
distraction, 15, 16, 120, 130
duration of task, 87

E

ear protectors, 117
Eindhoven, 171
energy saving, 93, 103
environmental effects, 7–8, 13–14, 15, 85–136
ergonomics, 1, 3, 4, 5–7, 139, 141, 153
Ergonomics, 42
ethology, 59–60
evaluation, 16, 17–18, 21–22, 157, 160
evaporation, 128
experimentation, 139, 144–145, 146, 164, 171

F

face the action, 62, 67
factories, 6, 12–13, 20–21, 35, 70–71, 72, 76, 80–81, 85, 123, 148–149
Fischer, D., 101, 110
Fisher, G.H., 122, 126
floor planning, 9, 13, 59, 69–83, 124, 168, 180
fluorescent light, 92, 93, 96, 97, 98, 100, 101, 102, 103, 107, 142
Flynn, John E., 62, 68, 102, 110
focused object, 123
foot rest, 40, 41, 52
Fotheringham, W.C., 178, 182
Fox, W.F., 130, 136
Francis, R.L., 80, 83
Freedman, J., 131, 136
functional layout, 71–73, 80
furniture, 14, 25, 30, 53, 58, 61, 63, 66, 154–155

G

General Electric, 96, 102, 111
general lighting, 93, 94, 103
glare, 8, 14, 87
Gorton, R.L., 132, 136
Gough, Harrison, 165
Grandjean, E., 126
graphics, 180–181
Griffitt, William, 131, 136
Guilford, Joy P., 106, 107, 111
Gundlach, E., 108, 111

H

Hall, E.T., 61, 68
hand activity, 27, 43, 48–51
Hanes, R.M., 108, 111
hardware, 27, 52–53
Hawthorne study, 148–149
health and safety, 1, 7, 11–13, 15, 16, 20, 52, 53, 82, 134, 155–156, 157–159 (*see also* Lighting health and safety, Sound health and safety, Thermal health and safety)
hearing loss, 113–117
heat and cold (*see* Thermal environment)
Heins, A.P., 89, 111
Helson, Harry, 7, 10, 106–107, 111
Hendrick, C., 68, 110
Hertzberg, H.T.E., 31, 57
Hewes, G.W., 34, 57
high intensity discharge lights, 97
Hill, A.R., 145, 161
Hitler, 66
home, 5–6, 13, 15, 20, 116, 123–125, 144
Hopkinson, Ralph, 19, 22
hospitals, 129, 133
hue, 104–109, 139–141
human factors (*see* Ergonomics)
humidity (*see* Relative humidity)

I

Illuminating Engineering Research Institute, 46
illumination (*also see* Lighting), 87–92, 95–96, 98–99, 101–102, 157, 159
illumination (in problem solving), 169
illumination standards, 15, 88–93
Illuminating Engineering Society (North America), 88, 99
incandescent light, 93, 97, 100, 102, 103, 107, 142
incubation, 168–169, 171–172
identification, 71
individual differences, 164–166
industrial engineering, 6, 13
information gathering, 69–72, 168, 171
intelligence, 165
interior (space) design, 1, 4, 5, 58, 168
interior ergonomics, 6
interviewing (*see* Questionnaires)

J

Jefferson, Thomas, 3–4
Jerome, C.W., 107, 111
Johns, E.H., 108, 111
Jones, R.D., 130, 136
Judd, D.B., 107, 111

K

Karr, A.C., 109, 111
Kaufman, John E., 88, 111
Keck, M.E., 143–144, 161
Kilty, T.K., 151, 161
Kinkade, R.G., 57
Kira, Alexander, 53, 57
kitchens, 145
Kleeman, Walter, 63–64, 68
Knapp, M.L., 60, 68
Konz, Stephan A., 72, 125, 126

Kroemer, K.H.E., 42, 57
Kryter, Karl D., 117, 119, 121, 126

L

Lansford, T., 10, 111
Lawrence, J.E.S., 60, 68
layout, 69, 76–82, 83 (*also see* Functional layout, Process layout, Product layout, Transactional layout)
Le Corbusier, 69
Learner, D.B., 42, 57
lighting, 7, 14, 15, 53, 62, 64, 76, 87–112, 143–144 (*see also* Illumination standards, General lighting, Lighting calculation, Lighting variability, Supplemental lighting)
lighting and performance, 92–95
lighting calculation, 95–98
lighting pleasantness, 102–104
lighting variability, 103
lighting health and safety, 87, 88–89
lightmeter, 90
lightness (*see* Value)
Lipscomb, D.M., 117, 126
living rooms, 17, 58, 60, 63, 64, 101, 110, 123
loudness, 114
Lowes, John L., 167, 176
lumens, 96–98
luminance, 87, 90, 91, 99, 100, 157
Luther, Martin, 21

M

Mackinon, 164
Macoubrey, C., 108, 111
Maltzman, Irving, 127, 132
Martyniuk, O., 68, 110
Maslow, Abraham, 19, 20, 22
McCain, C.N., 109, 111
McPherson, R.K., 129, 133, 136

mercury lights, 97
metal halide lights, 97
Miller, J.D., 119, 126
Mintz, N.L., 19, 22
mock-up, 146
model, scale, 146, 181
Morrison, 5
multidimensionality, 16
Munsell color system, 104–106
Mussolini, 66
Muther, Richard, 75, 83

N

National Institute for Occupational Safety and Health (NIOSH), 89
naturalistic observation, 142–143, 144
near point (*see* Viewing distance)
Nemecek, J., 126
Nevins, Ralph G., 132, 136
offices, 6, 13, 15, 17, 20, 46, 48, 58, 64, 65, 66, 71, 73, 74, 75, 82, 96–98, 103, 116, 119, 120, 122, 123, 124, 125, 142, 146, 147, 172–173, 179 (*see also* Open plan)
noise, 6, 12, 14, 15, 82, 113–126, 144, 157, 159
noise limits, 116, 123
noise masking, 124
noise types, 114

O

Occupational Safety and Health Act (OSHA), 12, 88, 116, 117
open plan, 120, 124, 145–146
orderliness (*see* Organization)
operations research, 169
organization, 16, 22, 160
originality, 163
Osborne, Alex, 172, 173, 176
Osgood, Charles E., 17, 23
Oxford, H.W., 28, 57

P

Pangrekar, Abhay, 93, 111
Parsons, Henry M., 149, 161
Payne, J., 150, 161
Payne, S.L., 151, 161
performance, 1, 7, 8, 11, 12, 13, 14, 16, 19, 20, 43, 52, 53, 58, 69, 70, 82, 85, 87, 113, 121, 155–156, 157 (*see also* Lighting and performance, Sound and performance, Thermal environment and performance)
Perkins, J.A., 177
personalization, 64, 65
phases in creativity and problem solving, 162, 166–170
photometer, 90, 157
physiological effects, 3, 6, 14, 16, 29, 35, 36, 38, 43, 48, 89, 143, 150
pitch, 114
pleasantness, 1, 7, 8, 11, 12, 13, 16–19, 20, 21–22, 87, 93, 155, 156, 157 (*see also* Lighting pleasantness, Sound pleasantness, Thermal pleasantness)
posture, 34–35, 38
potency, 18, 19
preparation, general, in creativity, 167, 170–171
presbycousis, 115
presbyopia, 43
presentation planning, 178
presentations and motivation, 178–180
presentations, making, 8, 9, 137, 177–182 (*see also* Presentation planning, Presentations and motivation, Rehersal, Themes)
privacy, 17, 63, 124, 142, 145, 180
problem recognition, 167–168, 171
problem solving (*see* Creativity, problem solving)
process layout, 70
product layout, 70
programming, 69, 70–76
Protestant (*see* Work ethic)
pseudo-experiment, 146
psychology, 3, 6, 16, 27, 142, 165, 170–171
psychosis, 165
Puritan (*see* Work ethic)

Q

questionnaires, 139, 149, 150–153, 156

R

radiation, 127, 128, 133, 135, 156
reactivity, 139, 148–153
reflectance, 87–91, 96, 100, 101, 104 (*see also* Value)
rehersal, 181
relative humidity, 127, 128, 131–132, 157
research, 6–7, 8, 139–161
research, applied and basic, 139, 142
research, role of, 139–142
research, types of, 142–146
restaurants and bars, 15, 59, 60, 62, 93, 95, 101, 103, 110, 123, 143
Rey, Paule, 140, 161
Robertson, W.G., 130, 136
Robinette, J.C., 57
Rohles, Frederick H., 131, 136

S

safety (*see* Health and safety)
sample (*see* Statistical inference)
saturation (color), 104, 105, 106, 107, 108, 109
schematic diagram, 76–78
schools (*see* Classrooms)
Schwartz, R.D., 161
seat back angle, 38, 39
seat base height, 40
seat base length, 40–41
seat comfort, 36, 42, 157, 159
seat distance and direction, 58, 61, 62, 63
seat reference point, 40
Seaton, R.W., 16, 23
seats, 14, 27, 34, 35–42, 56–57
Sechrest, L., 161
seeing, 43–48, 87, 91–93, 95

semantic differential, 16–19, 102
sex effects, 29, 31, 32, 41, 50
Shackel, B., 42, 57
Shakespeare, 127
Shipley, P., 57
signs, 13, 48, 149
simulation, 139
sitting forces, 36, 37
size and distance, apparent, 108, 109, 153–155
Smith, Patricia Cain, 111
Smith, Stanley W., 93, 111
social effects, 6, 25, 30, 58, 59, 60, 61, 62, 63, 65, 66
social group size, 61–62, 66–67, 68
sociofugal, 60
sociopetal, 60, 63
sodium light high pressure, 93, 97
sofas, 61
solution generation, 162, 168, 171, 172–174, 175
Sommer, Robert, 60, 61, 63, 68, 143, 161
sound, 8, 14, 76, 88, 113–126, 157
sound and health and safety, 114–118
sound and performance, 118–121
sound-level meter, 125
sound pleasantness, 124–125
space evaluation, 7, 9, 137, 139, 142, 145, 146, 148, 153, 155–160
space requirements, 69, 75–76
spaces, individual, 7, 13, 25, 27–57, 69, 157
spaces, large, 7, 9, 25, 59, 69–83
spaces, small, 7, 25, 58–68, 69
spaciousness, 16, 17, 21–22, 102, 153–155, 160
spatial visualization, 180–181
speech interference, 113, 118, 122–123
Spencer, T.J., 68, 110
Sprecher, Thomas B., 176
standing, 34, 35, 48, 50–51, 52
statistical inference, 139, 146–148, 151
stools, 41, 42, 50, 51
store, 13, 103, 142, 143
Suci, G.J., 23
Sucov, E.W., 88, 103, 112

Sullivan, Louis, 4
Summer, F.C., 108, 111
supplemental lighting, 93, 103
synectics, 174

T

Tannenbaum, P.H., 111
Taylor, 174
Taylor, L.H., 103, 112
themes, 179–180
templates, 78
temporary threshold shift, 117
tests, 145–146
territorility effects, 58, 59, 64–66
thermal comfort, 127, 129, 131–133, 134, 135, 139, 140, 147, 148, 149
thermal environment, 8, 12, 14, 15, 20, 53, 76, 85, 88, 127–136, 139, 140–141, 149
thermal environment and health and safety, 128–131
thermal environment and performance, 128–131
thermal pleasantness, 133–134
Timms, Kathie T., 176
Tinker, M.A., 92, 112
traffic, 72
transactional layout, 71–72
transient adaptation (*see* Glare)
transmittance, 90, 145

U

upholstery, 39–40

V

value, 104, 105, 106, 107, 108, 109
Van Cott, Harold P., 57
Van Wely, P., 34, 57
Veitch, R., 131, 136
verification, 169–170, 172
viewing angle, 27, 46–48, 99
viewing distance, 27, 43, 44, 45
Vinacke, W.E., 171, 176

vision (*see* Seeing)
visual task evaluation, 92

W

Wachsler, R.A., 42, 57
waiting and reception rooms and lounges, 59, 60–63, 155, 157
Walters, D., 144, 161
Watson, N., 22
Webb, E.J., 149, 161
Weixelman, John J., 149, 161
Welsh, A.S. and B.L., 118, 126
Wernick, R., 165, 176
Western Electric, 148
Westinghouse, 103
Weston, H.C., 92, 112
Wexner, L.B., 109, 112
Wheeler, J.A., 83
White, A.G., 66, 68
White, J.A., 80, 83
Whiting, C.S., 123, 174, 176
Williamson, Horace H., 76, 83
Wilson, G.D., 109, 112
windows, 53, 74, 76, 78, 141, 145, 154
Wing, J.F., 130, 136
Woodson, Wesley E., 49, 52, 53, 57
Wools, R.M., 9, 10, 141, 161
work, dynamic, 38
work ethic, 20–21, 35
workplace (*see* Spaces, individual)
work, static, 38, 43
work surface height, 27, 50, 51
Wright, Frank Lloyd, 125, 164
Wurtman, R.J., 89, 112

Y

Yerkes-Dodson effect, 120–121

Z

zonal cavity method, 95–96

I,